LIFE ON THE LINE

LIFE ON THE LINE

HOW TO LOSE A MILLION
AND SO MUCH MORE

KEVIN TWADDLE

WITH SCOTT BURNS

BLACK & WHITE PUBLISHING

First published 2012
by Black & White Publishing Ltd
29 Ocean Drive, Edinburgh EH6 6JL

1 3 5 7 9 10 8 6 4 2   12 13 14 15

ISBN: 978 1 84502 466 6

A CIP catalogue record for this book is available
from the British Library.

Typeset by Ellipsis Digital Ltd, Glasgow
Printed and bound by MPG Books Ltd, Bodmin, Cornwall

CONTENTS

ACKNOWLEDGEMENTS

There are so many people I would like to mention for their help and support through my life. I am going to mention a few by name, but there are so many more that I am indebted to that I could probably write another book on them alone. I would like to say thank you to everyone who has helped me along the way – before, during and also after my gambling – it is and always will be really appreciated.

I have to give special mentions to my wife, Jac, and my mum and dad, Anne and Derek. My mum and dad have been there for me every step of the way. I have taken them to hell and back, but it is testament to them that they are still by my side today. I look up to my mum so much, and my dad is the best friend – outside of Jac – and he has been my biggest supporter through my time at Gamblers Anonymous. I just want to say thank you to my mum and dad from the bottom of my heart for everything, and a hundred million apologies for everything I have put them through. Also I have to say thank you to Jac for being such a caring, loving and wonderful wife. You have helped to make my life what it is.

Other people who mean so much to me are my daughter Emma, my grandson Jack, my sister Nicola, and my niece Kelsa. All of Jac's family also fall into that category, especially her mum and dad, Margaret and Neil. They have provided Jac and me with unbelievable support and love.

GA has also played a massive part in my recovery. I would like to say a big thank you to all my GA friends all over Scotland, especially the people who attend or have attended my Thursday and Saturday morning meetings. You all mean so much to me.

There are a lot of individual people who have played a massive part in my recovery and time at GA. I would have to start with Bill and Marlene, who have been there for me from day one. There is also Tony, Jim, Andy, Arthur, Willie, Paul, Neil, Jamie and Matty, who are more like soul mates than friends to me.

Away from GA, there are also so many great people I also class as friends. There are my best men, Craig Dargo and Elliott Smith, who have been there for me through thick and thin and deserve medals for doing so! There is also Keith Salton, who was right behind me when I decided to go to GA, Will Dickson, Bob Murray and Grant Carnie – they all mean so much to me.

Also in the process of writing this book, I still can't believe that one of my heroes, Paul Merson, agreed to do the foreword for my autobiography. He is a player I always looked up to for the way he got on the ball and made things happen. He has also had his problems off the park, and I really appreciate him taking the time to provide a few words for my book.

I also have to thank my co-author, Scott Burns, who I have known since my time at Motherwell. He has given me some good press through the years and is a well-respected sports writer with the *Scottish Daily Express*. If it hadn't been for him then this book would never have become reality.

ACKNOWLEDGEMENTS

Scott and I would also like to thank Willie Vass for his help with the photographs and the picture element of the book, and Stuart Darroch for his assistance in the proofreading process.

Finally, I would like to thank Black & White Publishing for having the faith and belief to put my story into print and for allowing me to tell my story.

"A talented player whose career was undoubtedly troubled by his gambling addiction, Kevin is now providing valuable support to PFA Scotland as we educate players on the potential impact upon their profession that such an addiction can have."

Jack Ross
PFA Scotland

FOREWORD
BY PAUL MERSON

Out of all the addictions I have seen, I would say gambling is by far the hardest to try and overcome, as it is the only one where you don't need to put anything in your body. If you want to get drunk, you need to drink alcohol. If you want to get high, you need to take drugs. With gambling, you don't need to take anything because that addiction is already inside you.

Gambling is also different because it is almost impossible to uncover. When I was drinking a lot and I had been out all night, the manager and the coaching staff knew because they would see the state of me and smell the drink. It would be the same with drugs, but if I had been betting all night then nobody would have had the first clue because it is a more hidden addiction. You could walk down your main street and you could tell who was drunk or high, but you couldn't say who had a gambling problem. That is why it is such a dangerous addiction because nobody sees it or the damage it can cause.

Gamblers don't get a lot of help due to the secretive nature of the addiction, nobody knows if you are betting or not. Nobody finds out unless you get caught, come clean or all the doors close on your life and you hit rock bottom. It is only likely to be in one of those situations when a person will hold up their hands and admit they are in trouble. In my experience, you only stop gambling when you have no money and nothing left to gamble.

If you are an alcoholic and you are earning £100,000 a week, then it would be virtually impossible to spend it all on drink, but you could quite easily gamble it all. If you are a compulsive gambler then you could do that and a lot more on top, easily. The higher the stakes, the bigger the thrill. It doesn't have to be betting. You only have to look at Nick Leeson when he brought down Barings Bank. What he did was the equivalent of gambling. He made some big losses on some of his investments and he just kept chasing and ended up bringing a massive bank down.

Kevin will tell you that you could be £5,000 up and then lose your next £500 bet. It will then cost you another £6,000 to chase that £500 loss. Most people who don't have an addiction could walk away with £4,500, but not a compulsive gambler. They will go the opposite way.

I would say now that gambling is the biggest addiction of them all, especially in sport and in particular football. We live in a very different society today, even to when both myself and Kevin played. Social media is now massive and with mobile telephones now having cameras and internet access, footballers have to watch what they are doing because before they know it their picture could end up in the newspapers or on the internet. All the players know it is a lot easier just to go home and bet on football or horses and dogs, because they can do that without everybody else knowing their business.

Players at all the big clubs in Scotland and England are making big money, and the general public will argue there is no way you could bet five or six-figure sums. If you are a gambler and you are earning £40,000 a week then where is the buzz in having a £400 bet? If you are a compulsive gambler, you are more likely to gamble the full £40,000, or even more.

I, like Kevin, know how betting impacted on my football career. I remember a game when I was at Arsenal and we played the Danish team Odense in the European Cup Winners' Cup. We won the first leg out in Denmark. We totally battered them and we should have won more convincingly, and when I came back I started to think about the second leg at home. I checked the odds and we were 7–1 on to win, and I just thought that was the biggest give-me in the history of football. I put a fortune on us because I thought it would be the easiest money ever. We were all over them again, but they scored with five minutes to go and somehow managed to hold out for a draw. Everybody back in the Arsenal dressing room was really happy because we had qualified, but I was in absolute despair knowing I had done all my money in.

Instead of spending quality time with your family, you are looking on your phone and checking the scores and race results. I know betting stopped me from spending proper time with my kids. It is like an alcoholic – once you have that first drink you can't stop. If you are a compulsive gambler and you have put a bet on, then there is no way you could wait until you got home to find out the result. You want to know there and then.

If you speak to a compulsive gambler, as Kevin's story will tell, it isn't about the winning. You get the buzz from putting the bet on. That shows the craziness of being a compulsive gambler. Even if you do win, then all it does is give you even more money to bet. I will give you a prime example of that. I was at my mum and dad's house, and I had won a lot of money, something like £20,000, but I still had a face like thunder. My mum asked me what was wrong because I had won all that money and I still looked like I had lost the lot. My response was simple: 'Because there is nothing else to bet on because the bookies have closed.' That was about ten o'clock at night, but today with the internet you can bet twenty-four hours a day, seven days a week.

Gambling is that big that even *EastEnders*, one of the biggest shows on television, has had a betting theme as part of their storyline. Whenever you watch a football match there are betting adverts before the game, at half time and also at the final whistle. It is constantly thrown up in your face – 5–1 this and 7–2 this bet. The bookmakers and gambling companies make massive money from sport, and that is why they try and maximise their advertising opportunities.

It is very difficult for a compulsive gambler to try and stop betting because, as I have said, it is everywhere. I think if you want to stop and completely finish with gambling then you need help and support, because it is very hard to do it alone. That is where the likes of Gamblers Anonymous are so important. I know that, Kevin will tell you that and the thousands of people that GA have helped will also tell you something similar. GA gives your life a structure and lays out a plan as to how you can stop and stay away from the perils of gambling.

Some people reading this book will be shocked by some of the stories that Kevin is about to tell. I know I wouldn't be shocked by some of the things because I have done and experienced similar things to Kevin. I have been in that same movie. If you were in a GA meeting and told some of our stories then it would look like nothing compared to some of the horror stories that other people have gone through because of gambling.

Kevin deserves a lot of credit for writing this book. He has laid himself bare to help others. If one person reads this book and says, 'That is me and I don't want to end up like that,' then Kevin will have done his job. That would just be unbelievable. I hope and I am sure his story will help a lot more people who hopefully won't have to go down the road both Kevin and myself had to go down, because we both know it can be a long, long way back.

Paul Merson

INTRODUCTION

My name is Kevin Twaddle.

I am a husband, dad, granddad, son, uncle, businessman and former professional footballer. I am probably best remembered for my football career where I turned out for clubs like Motherwell, Hearts and St Johnstone. Most people will remember me as a happy-go-lucky winger, but underneath that false facade lay my deepest, darkest secret – I was a compulsive gambler.

There is no doubt that betting curtailed my football career, wrecked my life and led to me having suicidal thoughts and nearly ending it all. My addiction to gambling on horses, dogs and football, playing slot machines and betting on casinos tore my family apart, wrecked relationships, took over my life and completely destroyed and changed me as a person.

My betting took me to the verge of oblivion, racking up thousands of pounds worth of debt and turned me to theft and fraud. I blew in excess of £1 million in all my years of gambling, leaving myself with absolutely nothing, not even a future. I plumbed the depths of despair and I did some horrible things, especially to the people closest to me, and that guilt and shame is something that will live with me for the rest of my days. But I have not written this book for sympathy or pity. I know deep down those are the last things I deserve.

I hope by telling my story it will show that a gambling addiction, although it can never be overcome, can be self-managed. There are tens of thousands of people all cross the United Kingdom who have similar issues and will currently find themselves in the dark world that gambling left me in. It has been estimated that more than 350,000 people in the United Kingdom have a betting problem, although I wouldn't be surprised if that figure was substantially higher.

Gambling is big business. It is claimed that 73 percent of the British population bet at least once over the course of a calendar year. The turnover of the gambling industry in the British Isles in 2009 was a massive £8.7 billion and it gives employment to more than 200,000 people. It is something that starts off as fun, but for a lot of us, it quickly becomes an addiction. I am not just talking about football, dog or horse racing. There are different forms of gambling: from lottery tickets and scratch cards, to bingo, casinos and slot machines, while there has also been the recent explosion of online gambling.

I know that I am one of the lucky ones because I have been able, with more than a little help, to pick up the pieces and to turn my life around. I know there are a millions of people all over the world who haven't been as lucky. Maybe they didn't get the help and support I got, and there will be others who feel there is no escape from gambling.

I have, with the help of Gamblers Anonymous, my family and friends, been able to turn my life around. I no longer bet, I have not had a bet for more than six long years, but I know I will always remain as a recovering compulsive gambler. It never leaves you, but you just have to learn how to manage and deal with those impulses and urges to put money on something.

I have chosen to write this book not for money or financial gain but in the hope that my story can help anybody who is going through the same gambling nightmare that I had to endure, I certainly wouldn't wish what I went through on my worst enemy.

I just hope and pray that by baring my soul and putting my life on the line I will be able to help others. If one person reads this book and as a result turns their life around and stops gambling then it will have made it all worthwhile. That's why I have decided to be completely open and honest and to tell my story as it really was – a descent into a hell which had a devastating effect on me, my friends and my family, and from which I thought I would never escape.

Kevin Twaddle

1

SUICIDE: MY BEST BET?

The day Tuesday, 15 March 2005 is one that will live with me forever. I was ready to take my own life. I was going to commit suicide and end it all by taking a lethal cocktail of drugs.

It certainly wasn't the only time I had considered the end game. There had been a number of occasions when I had thought there was no other way out. I honestly felt that taking my own life was the only way I could escape from my gambling hell. I had thought about it a good few times in that year before I stopped gambling. My head had completely gone. I was being controlled by gambling. I felt like a puppet, and it had completely taken over me. I knew it was ruining my life, but I was powerless to stop it, my life was no longer my own.

There were no positives. If I am being honest, I couldn't see one single ray of light. My world had just become a dull and grey place with one thing at the centre of everything – gambling. It had taken everything I had physically and mentally (and more) and left me with nothing but misery, despair, anxiety, depression and, of course, a mountain of debt.

Suicide looked like the only feasible option. I had thought long and hard on many occasions about how I could kill myself. This wasn't just an isolated incident. Things were that bad. I had hit a real low point after I'd hung up my boots at St Mirren. My football career was over, and that left a huge void in my life. I was in a relationship and that kept me pretty stable for a while, but after that I was heading one way – down the road to wrack and ruin. My girlfriend and I had been together for three or four years, and probably in the final six months to a year of that relationship I had started to have suicidal thoughts.

I thought of taking my own life several times, I was in such a bad place. That day where I came closest I went out and bought loads and loads of pills with the plan to take them all with alcohol and to end things there and then. Paracetamols, Nurofen and aspirins – I bought them all, anything legal that I could get over the counter. I even went to various shops because there is a limit to what one pharmacist can sell to a customer. That was how broken and messed up I was; I was in such a dark place.

I got up in the middle of the night four or five times and sat downstairs with all the tablets on a table in front of me. That particular night, I even started to write a suicide note to my mum, dad and family. It was one open letter to them all. I started to jot down where I was in life and why I felt it was right to end things this way. I felt I had done so many wrongs to so many people. I got halfway down the page, read it and I just broke down crying. I had never really thought about my family or anybody else up to that point, but then I began to realise what taking my own life would have done to them.

The only thing that stopped me from killing myself was that I couldn't have put my mum and dad and the rest of my family through even more hell. They had suffered more than enough at my hands already. If I had killed myself then it was them and not me who would have been forced to live with the consequences, and my family would have had to live with it for the rest of their lives. That, I knew, wasn't fair.

Probably the one person who really stopped me doing it was my wee niece, Kelsa. Kelsa was born not long after my nana died, and I believe these things happen for a reason. I believe in karma. I'm in no doubt if Kelsa hadn't been there then I probably would have killed myself. I thought about my family as I looked at the pills on the table, but then I came to Kelsa, and I saw her wee face in my head and just couldn't go through with it.

I bought the pills but thankfully that was as far as I went. Some people might think I am a coward because I didn't go through with it, but I think I would have been more of a coward if I had killed myself. I would have left other people to pick up the pieces of something that was my own doing.

We have seen people like the Welsh national football team manager Gary Speed take their own life. Nobody knows what caused him to do what he did, but we all saw the devastation it caused to his family and to the football world. I have also witnessed the effects that suicide can have on people first-hand. My friend, Jokie Barr, hanged himself because he had a lot of personal problems in his life. That absolutely devastated me and took me back to where I had been in my life. Jokie had been through a hard time. He had just split up with a girl and there were also a couple of kids involved who he cared a lot about. I knew he had been going through hell, but I still didn't think he would do what he did and leave his family to try and pick up the pieces. I say that now because now I am in a very different place. It is so sad. I don't think I have cried as much in my life as I did that day we laid Jokie to rest. It left me totally demoralised and brought me back to where I had been. It was pretty surreal because it could have been my own funeral if I hadn't sorted my life out.

I suppose buying the pills shows what a bad place I was in. People say a suicide attempt is a cry for help. I can't say that was the case for me, because nobody knew the position I was in. Absolutely nobody, and it's not the sort of thing you are going to speak to people about. Looking back, though, it's astonishing to think how much of my life was hidden away from people who were close to me but had no idea what was really going on.

At my lowest during those times, an overdose wasn't the only suicide method I considered. I don't drive but I even had a daft notion of turning the steering wheel when I was in somebody else's car, so not only was I looking to take my own life but I could quite easily have taken somebody else's into the bargain. It was a ridiculous thought, but I was so desperate that it was one idea that crossed my mind. I also considered going to the Forth Road Bridge and just throwing myself off it because I just thought I would have been better out of the way. Every time I considered suicide my mind always flashed back to my family, and in particular Kelsa. I just couldn't put them through it. I just couldn't. If I knew that it wouldn't have affected them, then I would have done it in a heartbeat.

I have known people from my time at Gamblers Anonymous who have actually gone on and taken their own lives. It is absolutely heartbreaking and the carnage they leave behind can be horrendous. But when you are in that state of mind there are times when you can't see the light at the end of the tunnel. You are in this dark place and you feel it would be best for all concerned just to end things. It is a fact that suicide rates are much higher amongst people with known gambling problems.

Thankfully, I had a wee bit of common sense about me. I couldn't leave the trail of destruction behind for everybody else to deal with. I had put them through more than enough. I also have to say if I hadn't faced up to my problems and gone to GA then I probably would have tried to take my life again. Going to GA is the best thing I have ever done in my life and enables me to have everything I have in my life today – family, friends and business – but the biggest thing is just being here and knowing I still have life. Without that support I wouldn't be here still breathing today.

Gambling stripped me bare. It completely took over my life. It left me in the depths of despair. And the one thing you need to gamble is money. Whenever I had a bit of money it was only going one way, and when I was skint I started to dream up all sorts of schemes to get my hands on cash. I have put some massive individual bets on during my time when I was right on the edge. I have blown an absolute fortune but come the end, instead of big-money bets, I was punting the equivalent of children's weekly pocket money because that is all I had left.

Gamblers always need more money and some of the thoughts and brainwaves I had to get it would have put a Hollywood scriptwriter to shame. I was so messed up that I even considered robbing banks and post offices. I actually looked into a few post offices that could have been options. I was being deadly serious – it wasn't just a case of idly thinking about it. I also went into the nuts and bolts of how I was going to do it and even considered getting some well-connected people in on the act. I probably would have tried to get somebody else to do it. I had considering doing it myself, but I don't know if I really had the guts to go through with it. Thankfully, I never went that far because I fear if I had then I might never have got my life back. I was already stealing from my family at that time and I had no intention of paying them back, but I just didn't see anything wrong with what I was doing. I could always manage to justify it in my own head to make sure I had enough for another bet, no matter where the money was coming from.

At one point I even thought about trying to sell drugs to make money. I had never touched drugs in my life but I was prepared

5

to deal in them just to make a quick buck so I could continue betting. That was all back in 2005. I was completely out of control. I had fallen so far that I probably never thought what I was considering was illegal or wrong. I was at the point where I would have done anything, anything that would have got me money, legal or otherwise. If it had meant stealing my mum and dad's house and leaving them out on the street, then I would have done it. I was in that bad a place. I was completely desperate.

I am just glad that day and those schemes never turned out the way I had planned, otherwise I wouldn't be here to tell my story.

2

HITTING ROCK BOTTOM

I may have thought long and hard about taking my own life, but unbelievably, I still had a lot further to fall. I continued to have suicidal thoughts of how I could escape from it all and my ever-worsening gambling problem. At that point, gambling was my life and nothing else mattered. Yes, I had thought long and hard about killing myself but I didn't do it, and by the next day I was still ready to put that next bet on. Betting wasn't making me happy, it was just helping me feed my addiction. I was in this deep dark cycle of despair from which I could see no way out. I was borrowing, stealing and begging money just so I could put on that next bet. It was no way for anybody to live their life – if you could call it a life.

I know it may sound crazy, but even at this low point I was still some way from hitting rock bottom. That was to come six or seven months after I had contemplated ending it all. The date 4 October 2005 turned out to be my real day of reckoning. That was when the penny finally dropped, I realised I had a serious illness and I had to do something about it fast. I had to confront my worst fears before gambling ruined my life and those of the people closest to me. I knew I had a problem. I had done some serious and horrible things just to get the money to bet, things that still embarrass me today and even now it is difficult to talk about some of the entries in my hall of shame. The impulse to gamble was dragging me further and further down. It didn't matter how far I had fallen, I would never face up to my problems. I knew I had a problem but I just couldn't face up to it.

Like any addict, I was in denial. I felt I was in control of the situation even though nothing could have been further from the truth. I was like a runaway train thundering to the end of the track, and I honestly didn't think there was anything or anyone on earth who could have stopped me gambling. Thankfully, I was wrong on that one. There was somebody who could finally make me see the error of my ways. I have a former girlfriend to thank. I would like to name her, but that would be unfair. I have put her through so much and now both our lives have moved on. She is now in her own relationship and doing well for herself. We are no longer in contact, but I know I will be forever indebted to her for helping me see the light and for giving me the starting point from which to rebuild my life.

I was with her in a taxi on the way home from a night out and were heading back to her place. Suddenly she turned to me and said, 'Don't bother coming back to the flat. You are not getting in.'

I replied, 'What?'

Then she started crying and getting really emotional. She then opened up and said, 'You need to get a grip of yourself. You need help and you need to get yourself sorted out. You have absolutely nothing in your life. You have achieved so much, but you have absolutely nothing to show for it. You need to get yourself sorted out because your life is nothing more than a sham. Your life is nothing. It has been a complete waste.'

The words felt cruel and cutting and hit me like a sledgehammer. It was crushing to hear my life put so bluntly. It probably hit me even harder because I didn't see it coming. I can see now what my gambling was doing to her and the people close to me, but not at that point. I was too wrapped up in that next bet and I honestly didn't think there was a problem between us – that was how deluded I was. Of course, she was spot on with what she said. Bang on the money. Although the one thing my former girlfriend never actually mentioned was my gambling. We hadn't even had an argument, but that night was where she hit breaking point and thought enough was enough. Now, with hindsight, I know I can't blame her. The only surprise was that things didn't blow up sooner.

It was that night my world started crumbling around me. There comes a point in your life where you think, 'Wow', and it happened to me that evening. It is hard to put into words. Even attempted suicide didn't have such an impact on me, but those words from my then-girlfriend hammered home some harsh truths, and they were things that I needed to hear. It was long overdue. Nobody had been brave enough, nobody close enough anyway, to challenge me and tell me I had a problem. Sitting in the taxi listening to what I was being told, it is actually hard to explain how I felt. It was like an out-of-body experience. Everything just drained from me. I realised at that point I needed help. I had to face my demons and finally grow up and become a man and I had to stop running away from life. I could no longer deny I had a problem.

People say in life that sometimes you have to be cruel to be kind and, for me, that night proved to be the case. I sat in the taxi and listened to every word she had to say, even though they cut me to the core. It had the desired effect – it finally got me to open my eyes to the state I had got myself into. I said to myself, 'You know, she is absolutely right. My life is an absolute mess.' I had to take a serious look at myself.

I went home to my mum and dad's house in Danderhall, just outside Edinburgh, and that Thursday night I just lay in my bed and my heart broke. I cried most of that night and well into morning. For the first time in my life I had finally realised I had issues. I needed to get help. Everything spun round in my head, and I knew I had to admit defeat. My life had spiralled completely out of control.

I had put my girlfriend through so much with my gambling and had not only destroyed my own life but dragged her and so many of my family members and friends down with me. That night in the taxi was the tipping point for her. It had just been a long and frustrating build-up that came to a head that night. I think she knew that I was never going to change as a person. I was a gambling addict and she had seen what it had done to my life. I had been a footballer earning good money, but my betting habits had stripped me of everything and had left me with nothing. It had changed me as a person, and it certainly wasn't for the better.

What my girlfriend told me hit me hard. It made me sit up and take notice of the path of destruction I was racing down. When people go to Gamblers Anonymous for the first time they will always go back to that point in their life that made or forced them to come through the doors for that first meeting. Whether that is a suicide attempt or wherever gambling has taken them. My defining moment was in that taxi that night. I was somewhere I had never been before. I had sunk so low, I had hit rock bottom and I knew then I couldn't go any further down.

The good thing, from my point of view, is that those words had come from somebody close to me. Somebody I cared about and loved, although I know at times the way I acted and treated her, she would find that hard to believe. Maybe if it hadn't come from her or somebody I respected, then I wouldn't even have paid the slightest bit of notice because I always knew better.

It is hard to explain just how low I was at that time in my life. It is almost impossible to put into words. But that was where I was in the taxi that night. That was how I felt when I saw my life for what it was. I was a broken man and a shell of a person. I had to be broken; otherwise I know I would never have agreed to seek help. I had racked up thousands of pounds' worth of debt with people I shouldn't have been getting involved with. I had reneged on loans and I was looking at a possible jail sentence for fraud. I had also stolen and deceived a lot of people out of a lot of money, including friends and family. I had even considered serious crime and taking my own life. I don't know if gambling could have taken me any lower. Who knows? Maybe it could have.

Hopefully now I will never find out.

3

A NOT SO LUCKY COUPON

Where exactly did my gambling hell begin? I can always remember my first bet. I was only thirteen and I was with my dad. He told me to pick one football team from each section and he would put a coupon on for me. I picked my teams and my dad paid my stake and put it on. So you could imagine how excitedly I listened to the radio and then watched the full-time results come through on the television. One by one my selected results came in. It wasn't as if I had been studying the form, it was sheer beginner's luck. I won £84 from that first bet, although because I was still a minor my dad had to pick up my winnings for me. But I will never forget the buzz of that first win – it felt like a lottery win for this young school kid.

I started thinking to myself, 'This is easy. I could make a lot of money betting.' I started to put my own coupons on and it didn't take long to move away from the football to dog and horse racing. I still wasn't old enough to bet, so I would need to get other people to go into the bookies and put the bets on for me.

I suppose you want to know how I funded my early gambling? Well, I delivered newspapers and suddenly those wages went from football cards to giving me money to finance my new pastime. There were times when the good residents of Danderhall didn't even get their morning newspapers because I had gambled their money away. So I think it's fair to say that I was starting to get addicted even that early on. I would be going round to my customers' front doors and telling them bare-faced lies, like there weren't any papers left in the shop because I had been too late in getting there. I would then make my apologies and tell them that I would make sure they got their papers the following week, but even then there were no cast-iron guarantees.

I would beg, borrow and steal to make sure I had money to punt. I look back now and I see the problems, but back then I didn't think it was an issue, it was more a bit of innocent fun. I never saw it as the start of something, it was just a bit of light-hearted relief and the chance to try and win some money.

I even gambled at school. I would play cards and pitch and toss, where you had to throw money at a wall and the person closest would win. I was a really bad loser, even back then, regardless of whether they were classmates or friends, I would argue and go into the huff with them if I lost. I hated losing and I had to win all the time. At times, I was just the brat from hell. Even when I was playing cards with my mum or my nana I would never accept coming off second best, and if I did then I would cause absolute uproar in the house. I would smash tables and anything I could get my hands on because I was such a bad loser.

Family games of cards and playground challenges soon weren't enough to satisfy my urges. I wanted to win big money and that obviously came with bigger risks. There used to be a bookies in Danderhall where I would spend a lot of my time. It was run by Gordon and Kelvin and it was handy – probably too handy – because we used to stay right beside their shop. It was perfect for me. I used to jump over the back fence and I was there, at the wee bookies' hut. It was just far too convenient.

It is quite funny because my dad used to come down to put his coupons on. I used to leave friends like Matty Wright, who I still know today, out front so they could run in and let me know if he was coming down, giving me time to sneak out the back without getting seen or, even worse, caught. I was underage and even when I did come of age, I couldn't be seen in the bookies by my dad because it just led to friction and arguments in the house. And by that time, I had already started to steal from my mum.

My dad put that first coupon on for me, and I think he still remains on a guilt trip to this day over it. He even stopped gambling for a wee while and refused to go to York or his race meetings with the boys because of me. He felt he was letting me down if he continued to gamble and I had to convince him that it was me and not him who had the problem.

I am happy for him to bet whenever or on whatever he wants. I would love to join him for a wee bet on a Saturday, but unfortunately I know I can't.

4

MESSI – WITH A PAINTBRUSH

I was a really good football player when I was a youngster. I played for Edina Hibs in Edinburgh and I did pretty well when I was there. I was a flying winger. I had pace to burn and loved to knock the ball past defenders and then race past them. Pace was my main attribute, although I was also decent on the ball.

I quickly attracted interest from quite a few senior clubs from Scotland, England and even Europe. The Dutch giants Ajax were also keen to sign me. I had gone across to Holland with Edina Hibs and played in a youth tournament there. I did reasonably well, and that is where I caught the eye of one of the Ajax scouts. He asked one of the other boys and me to go across and play with, train and progress through their academy. We are talking about one of the biggest clubs in Europe at that time, a team who had lifted the European Cup and had blooded Dutch legends like Johan Cruyff, Dennis Bergkamp, Patrick Kluivert and Edwin van der Sar. When I think back, it was a once in a lifetime opportunity. I could have gone out there and received one of the best footballing educations I could have ever asked for. Most young boys in my situation would have jumped on the first flight out there – but not me. I was still only sixteen and I wasn't interested in leaving home. You could say I chose Danderhall and Edina Hibs over Ajax. I felt I was too young and didn't think I could survive without my family. If I had gone and made a fist

15

of it, then my life could have ended up totally different and maybe without a lifetime of gambling, but you make decisions in life and you can't look back, you just have to stand by them.

I kept playing with Edina when another team closer to home came calling, although it wasn't the club I had been hoping for. I would have given my right arm to play for Hearts, but it was Hibs who made their move. I was a diehard Jambo, maroon and white to the core. How could I possibly go to Easter Road? I thought I just couldn't go there. A few people spoke to me – family, friends and some of the people at Edina – and they said I should give Hibs a go. I was told that I should go down and train and see what happened from there. So against my better judgement, I decided to go to Easter Road. I started training there when I was sixteen, but I wasted my time and the time of the Hibs coaches. I acted like a complete idiot. I was a Hearts fan and was so anti-Hibs and all their players it was unbelievable. I was sixteen, but I acted like a spoiled five-year-old. I had an obvious chip on my shoulder, although I still did ok on the field, so much so that Hibs offered me a professional contract. It should have been a no-brainer, but this is me we're talking about.

I decided there was no way I was going to sign for Hibs. I turned them down flat, and this time there was to be no change of heart. It was one thing to play for Hibs youths but another thing altogether to sign professional forms for them. That showed the height of my immaturity and stupidity. I think 85 percent of my decision came down to the fact I was a Hearts fan. I don't think I actually gave my football career a second thought. I could never have seen myself pulling on that green and white jersey. I had been everywhere watching the Hearts and I just couldn't have done it, regardless of the reasons why I went to watch my boyhood heroes. I probably couldn't have gone to a better club with better people than Hibs, but I didn't see it that way. Ben McGovern was at Edina Hibs and he had close links with the Easter Road club. He was never away from my door, trying to persuade me to go to Hibs, but he quickly found out he was fighting a losing battle.

If that decision wasn't crazy enough, I ended up walking away from the game altogether. And instead of playing, the focus of my football turned solely to being a fan again. I followed Hearts all over the world. People thought I was a massive Hearts supporter, but looking back, was I really? Probably the main reason why I went to watch so many games wasn't because of the football but the fact it would allow me to gamble the length and breadth of the country. We would spend hours on the bus travelling and playing cards for money, and the reality is, that was as big if not bigger than the football to me. I went to Aberdeen, Dundee and even to European games – the further away, the better – because I would get longer to play cards.

Looking back now, did I actually want to go to the games? Probably not. I just wanted to be gambling. Even then it would get me into bother because I used to try and cheat so I could win, but I couldn't even do that right. I was absolutely useless. Now I watch football and I have done a bit of coaching and I realise what the game actually means to me. This is a guy who was a professional footballer for eleven years. It was such a massive part of my life, but it really wasn't what it should have been. I now enjoy my football, and I just wish I could have said the same during all the time I was playing.

I had the chance to go to Hibs or even Ajax, but instead of learning the trade of a professional footballer I went out and got myself a trade as a painter and decorator. At least I was good at football. I was a terrible painter and tradesman. I wasn't interested in the slightest. I only did it because it was an apprenticeship. I had no interest in becoming a painter, but it was a job and would provide me with a steady stream of income. Rollands Limited, a big company in Edinburgh, offered me my apprenticeship and I started there when I was sixteen. They were one of the biggest firms in the capital and my dad worked with them until they went out of business recently. I only got a job there because my dad's uncle, Jimmy Mitchell, was the managing director. He was one of two directors who looked after the business. I was put on the side of the other director, Willie McEwan. Willie now has his own painting business and he has also helped sponsor my pool-playing career. He used to be my boss but now he is a good friend.

Willie remained my travelling foreman for four or five years. I got on really well with him because he was right into his football. He used to take the young boys at Hibs and was massive down there. He then left Easter Road, but he took a big interest in me when I started to play football again. He had pictures of me when I turned professional up in his office. Wee daft photographs, like me climbing up a ladder alongside the headline 'Climbing the Ladder to Success'.

But even with a great boss, things didn't seem right. Even after my first month at Rollands, I said to myself, 'What are you doing here? You should be playing football and earning some real money.' I knew it was a good job but I had no real interest, even though I was working next to my dad. I couldn't paint, paper or master any of the basic skills you needed to be good at the job. I was the worst ever. How I ever finished my apprenticeship, I will never know.

Even though I got to the end of my apprenticeship, gambling also stole it away from me, as I didn't apply myself as much as I should have because I was so focused on gambling. For example, when I was an apprentice I used to take the lunch orders and then go and pick them up. I would have umpteen things on it from fish suppers to sandwiches, sausage rolls and pies from the baker. I remember we were working on a job in Stirling. I left the office we were working on and headed off down the street. I never even got as far as the baker, newsagent or fish and chip shop. The first thing I clocked on the way down the road was an amusement arcade with slot machines. I ended up spending all the lunch money on the one-armed bandits. Even though my dad was working on the same job as me, I then tried to cover up my lies by scraping the side of my face against a wall to make it look like I had been attacked. I got back to the office where we were working, looking a lot worse for wear. I laid it on thick that I had been jumped and these two guys had taken all the money. The guys were genuinely concerned for my welfare. They couldn't believe somebody could have done something like that, and one or two of the guys were even ready to go out to try and find the offenders.

I had done all that because I had gambled £20 or £30 away on slot machines. I was still a teenager, and already I had started to show all the classic symptoms of a gambling addict. I would lie and mislead people and even try to con people out of their hard-earned money. I pulled that trick quite a few times until my workmates started to become wise to my wide-boy ways, and even my dad knew what was going on. I know I severely embarrassed him, although I didn't give a hoot. The boys knew I was gambling their money away, too, and they started to lock me in cupboards so I would learn my lesson. They knew by the end what I was up to, but it still didn't stop me.

I worked there for four years before I left Rollands to go and work with my mate Ecky Stewart. He had his own business. One of my best mates, Jamie Murray, knew I was a half-decent footballer and around that time asked, 'Instead of going to watch

19

Hearts, why don't you come and play for Danderhall amateurs?' I decided to give it a go and I played for Danderhall for a season. I ended up scoring fifty-six goals, which is still a record at the club. That was the big thing, however, I was also getting a real buzz and enjoyment from playing the game again.

Ecky was playing for the junior team Dunbar United. He told me that I should come and join them because I would get a signing-on fee of £200, a pair of boots and if I did well I would get myself in the paper on a regular basis. I thought, 'Wow, where do I sign? Forget the boots, forget the paper, just give me the money.'

I went down, signed and had bet the money away before I had even been at my first training session. I also ended up selling the boots to get myself even more cash. It was quite embarrassing because when I went down for my first game I had this old pair of boots with me. The officials asked why I wasn't wearing my new boots, and I made all sorts of excuses.

Thankfully, the lack of gloss on my boots didn't deter me. I went out and played really well for Dunbar. I scored ten goals in my first nine games, and after that St Johnstone came in and offered me a trial. Despite my efforts not to use my footballing abilities, it seemed that there were still people out there who were keen to help me really make something of myself.

5

ST JOHNSTONE:
MY FIELD OF DREAMS

I still recall the day of my St Johnstone trial. I was working with Ecky Stewart, painting and decorating in Edinburgh. After I had finished I went home to get my boots and gear and rushed back up to Dunfermline for the game. I didn't even have time for a shower. I just stuck a tracksuit on, and I didn't even realise that I was still splattered with paint. I felt really embarrassed when I walked into the away dressing room at East End Park. All the rest of the St Johnstone players were suited and booted, apart from me and another triallist. I went and sheepishly took a seat in the corner, but Paul Sturrock clocked me right away. He joked, 'Nice to see you've made an effort, big man.' It didn't take long for the St Johnstone players to get in on the act either. I had a laugh and joke about it, but inside I was fuming. I thought, 'Why am I getting slaughtered? I've been out trying to earn an honest crust.'

I had made an early impression on my teammates but I knew it was out on the pitch where I really had to catch the eye. It was a whole new experience for me. The Saturday previously I had played for Dunbar at Bonnrigg in front of 350 people. Suddenly, I was at a senior Scottish ground getting ready to play a reserve game with experienced top-level professionals. Players

I had watched on the television every other week or read about in the papers. I looked around the St Johnstone dressing room and there were guys like Peter Davenport, Tommy Turner, Harry Curran, Ian Ferguson and Allan Preston. They were all top-team regulars but had been forced to play in the reserve game because the manager had been unhappy with their performances the previous Saturday against Clydebank.

The manager told me I was starting. I played up front along-side a young striker called Alan Morgan. He eventually went on to sign for Blackburn Rovers, but when he picked up a bad injury, that pretty much curtailed his senior career. I played for seventy minutes in the game and by that point I was absolutely gone. I could hardly run, and I pretty much needed an oxygen mask just to walk off the pitch when I was substituted. I was absolutely spent but I had been pleased with the way I had played. I felt I had done really well, although I never scored. The highlight was setting up our first goal for Alan in our 2–1 win. I had gone out and played my natural game. I was a centre-forward who ran the channels, looking for midfielders or defenders to play me in. I was also pretty quick, so that was another strong asset that went in my favour. The other triallist also did okay in the game and so we were both keen to learn our fate.

The manager came into the dressing room and told the rest of the boys that they had put on a decent performance and said well done to me and the other triallist. He addressed the group and said, 'You will all be in tomorrow morning for a jog and a stretch, while the rest of the first-team boys are out training.' He never said a word to me. I just got changed and got myself ready to go, still not knowing what was going to happen.

I was just about to walk out the door when I saw the manager speaking to the other triallist outside. They had a short chat and then the boy walked away. The manager then came into the dressing room a few minutes later and said, 'Kevin, can I have a word with you?' He took me outside and we stood at the halfway line at East End Park.

I still recall what he said to me. 'I thought you did really well,' he claimed. 'You are really quick for a big lad, and you have a decent touch, although you are terrible in the air and your fitness levels are absolutely diabolical. I am not going to hold your fitness against you because I know you are coming from junior football, and it is a long way short of top-level football. That is expected.'

He then asked me how I thought I had done. I told him I felt I had done okay but I could still do a lot better. I also told him I was disappointed that I hadn't scored, although I didn't really have any clear-cut opportunities. He listened and then said, 'You will need to get in touch with Dunbar because I feel we can maybe work with you. There is a deal here for you, if you want it. How would you feel about full-time football?'

I was standing there absolutely stunned. I just stood there and thought, 'Yes, that would be absolutely amazing.'

I walked out of East End Park that night as proud as punch. Some of the officials from Dunbar had been at the game. Tony McLaren and Alex McLaren, who were the manager and chairman at Dunbar, had come up to the match, along with Ecky Stewart. They were all waiting outside for me. I went out and told them the good news. I said, 'St Johnstone want to sign me. You have to come up to Perth tomorrow night with my parents to see if we can get a deal done.' They were all really pleased for me, and I think we were all pretty excited about the prospect of going up to Perth for talks.

Any thoughts of me becoming a Big-Time Charlie were quickly knocked out of me, however. I said to Ecky, 'I am not sure if I will be working tomorrow.' He replied, 'We have got a big job to do so, believe me, you will be working.' I did put a shift in that Thursday, although I finished slightly earlier, around two o'clock in the afternoon, so that I could get properly washed and changed before I headed to McDiarmid Park.

I felt really nervous as we got to the ground, just thinking I could be playing professional football there. St Johnstone were in the First Division but they were still one of Scotland's bigger clubs. I couldn't believe that I was about to swap my paintbrush and overalls to play professional football. I knew I was lucky to be getting a second chance. There aren't that many guys who slip through the net as a youngster and come back to get another chance. I will always be extremely grateful to Paul Sturrock and St Johnstone for giving me that opportunity.

I went in and we met with Paul and a few of the officials. It gave me a real buzz to finally be getting the chance to become a full-time footballer. The manager could have offered me £50 a week – well, okay, maybe £100 a week, because, remember, I still had my betting to fund. My side of the deal was agreed pretty quickly. I was given something along the lines of £300 a week before my transfer fee with Dunbar was thrashed out. They ended up getting £6,000, which still remains a club record fee to this day. I had only been at Dunbar for nine games. They had given me a pair of boots and £200, so it wasn't a bad return from their point of view.

I signed my contract with St Johnstone, and then Paul Sturrock told me I wouldn't be anywhere near the first team until I got myself fit. He said I would probably be two or three months away because my fitness levels were that bad. He also told me I would need to move up to Perth. When I heard that, it sent a shiver down my spine. I suddenly had thoughts of, 'Do I really want to do this? Despite the way I have treated my family, I am a real home bird.'

The manager told me it wouldn't be that bad and I could stay down in Edinburgh at the weekend after our games. The situation was far from ideal, but then reality hit me. Perth was only an hour away, it wasn't as if it was Holland or somewhere thousands of miles away. I had already missed the boat once, and I knew I was now standing in the last-chance saloon if I wanted to become a professional footballer. I realised that if I had to move to Perth for a bit, then it was a small sacrifice to make. It wouldn't be forever, and given a straight choice between football and painting, then there really only was ever going to be one winner.

So I agreed and signed. I got my pictures taken for the local paper, the *Perth Advertiser*, and did a few photographs for the club sponsor Famous Grouse. The gaffer then told me that I could come up and watch the first team on the Saturday. They were due to play Dunfermline at McDiarmid Park. So come the Friday night I thought I might go out and have a drink or two to celebrate my new job. So I was in the flat getting dressed and ready to go out with Jill, my girlfriend at the time, when the phone went.

I picked it up and the guy on the other side said, 'Hello, it is Paul Sturrock.'

I just laughed and replied, 'Ha ha, very good,' and I put the phone down and went into the bathroom again to continue getting ready. I then told Jill if that phone goes again not to answer it because it will be somebody on the wind-up.

She said, 'I will have to get it. What if it is somebody looking for me?'

A minute or so later the phone rang again and Jill answered it. Once again the man said he was Paul Sturrock and he wanted to speak to me. Jill told me, 'It is Paul Sturrock, and he wants you on the phone now.'

I thought, 'Enough is enough,' and I took the phone off Jill and hung up.

Seconds later, the phone went again. I picked it up and before I could get the chance to say anything, the voice on the other side said, 'You better listen to this. It is Paul Sturrock here.' I was still in denial and asked him to prove it.

He said, 'Well I know you played in a reserve game on Wednesday and you were up the following day to sign at McDiarmid Park with your parents.'

It was then the penny dropped. I thought to myself, 'What an idiot. It had been Paul Sturrock all along!' I had been certain it was one of my pals on the wind-up, but I had to eat humble pie and apologise.

Once we had got our little misunderstanding out of the way, I then thought the manager was at the wind-up himself. He said, 'We have quite a few injuries so we need you to play on Saturday. If you come up you can get your medical before the game and then you can come in and meet all the boys. You might even be on the bench.' He signed off with, 'It is not as if you would have been going out tonight anyway, now that you are a professional footballer.'

I then told a little white lie when I replied, 'No, gaffer, I was just going to be sitting here watching the television.' I came off the phone and told Jill, and she was absolutely delighted. I then had to go and phone all my family and friends to tell them the good news. For the record, I didn't go out that night.

I went up to Dunfermline early that Saturday morning. I did my medical and then I just remember sitting in the dressing room in my own wee world. I was looking round in total amazement that I was in the company of so many top players. I had also done a bit more homework on Peter Davenport, and it was unbelievable just to be in the same company as somebody like him, never mind the same team. This was a guy who had played under Brian Clough at Nottingham Forest and had also starred for Manchester United and Middlesbrough. Before I knew it, Paul Sturrock had come in and started to read out his starting XI. It was such a surreal moment for me, so much so that I didn't even take in what the team was. The manager started marking out his team and his tactics on this whiteboard, and it was then I knew I wasn't starting. He went through his team talk and then named his substitutes. I still didn't think I was going to be involved until he announced I was to be the final player on his bench.

I quickly got stripped and went out and did my warm-up with the team. I can't explain how I felt, it was amazing. It might only have been a league match between St Johnstone and Dunfermline, but to me it felt like a World Cup final. I was like a wee kid in a toyshop by the time I had taken my seat on the bench. Everything was so new to me and everywhere I looked I thought, 'Wow'. It was almost heavenly until the St Johnstone assistant manager, John Blackley, quickly shattered that illusion.

Dunfermline scored and then they doubled their lead. Our experienced defender, Paul Cherry, was playing at right-back. The manager started to give him pelters, and then John got off the bench and started going ballistic at him as well. I just sat there in total shock. John was tearing shreds off him, but all credit to Paul, because he gave as good as he got. That didn't help John's mood. He was raging and stomping up and down the dugout. I remember sitting thinking, 'These guys are mental. What have I done here? What have I let myself in for?' I was still young and relatively naive and I thought to myself, 'If he was to speak to me like that I will end up in tears.'

Things didn't get any better. We went in 3–0 down at half time. John and Paul took their argument back to the dressing room. I tried to stay as far away from them as was humanly possible. I wasn't wanting involved. John gave Paul it tight. He left him without a name, and this time Paul knew better than to say anything back. In fact, I have to say I felt pretty intimidated. On day one of my professional career I found out how cruel a place a football dressing room could be.

I once again started to have doubts. I thought, 'Am I tough enough for this?' Then I started to think, 'How can I get out of this?' I definitely didn't think I was cut out or tough enough for professional football. Even the prospect of getting the overalls and paintbrush out again didn't seem like such a bad idea after all. I managed to get through that half-time interval without catching anybody's attention, and I sneaked back out onto the bench. I was just sitting watching the game, still thinking, 'Is this really for me?'

Then ten minutes into the second half, Paul Sturrock turned to me and said, 'Right, go and get warmed up. You are going on.' I just looked at him and asked, 'Me?' The manager turned around and said, 'Of course I am talking to you, soft lad.' I went and got warmed up. The match was played at 100 miles an hour, and I thought just five minutes would do me. Minutes later, I got the shout and I was sent into the lion's den. I was put on at centre-forward and ended up directly against the late Dunfermline captain Norrie McCathie, who was a good, solid, experienced defender. I might have had reservations before I stepped out on the pitch, but to be fair, as soon as I got involved in the action I felt right at home. I thought I did quite well, although we still ended up losing 3–0. I just went out and ran myself into the ground. I didn't show a lot in terms of ability, but I did put a right shift in.

I felt reasonably pleased with myself as we went back to the dressing room. I got there and then Paul Sturrock walked in and nearly took the door off its hinges. He started going mental at the team. Once again, I just sat there, praying he wouldn't turn his sights on me. He went right through the team and then he turned to me. I thought, 'Oh, my God. Please, don't say anything,' while all the time I thought I am going to get it here. He said, 'See him? He has come to this football club covered in paint. He came in today and ran about daft. He gave me everything. That is what football is to me. He appreciates football because he knows what it is like to be out grafting in the real world. Half of you guys in here don't know you're living.' He was paying me a compliment and it was a boost to my confidence, but at the same time I thought the rest of my teammates are going to hate me even more. I never said a word after the manager was finished. I just got showered and changed and tried to get out as quickly as I could so I could meet my dad and two of my friends, Billy Aitchison and Billy Dickson, who had come to the game.

Before I left, a few of the Edinburgh-based boys arranged to give me a lift up to Perth on the Monday. Come that day, I was hardly in the car five minutes and the boys started to slaughter me for being the gaffer's blue-eyed boy. I then walked into the dressing room and all the banter started again, all good-natured stuff like, 'Should you not be away painting somebody's living room?' and 'When are you going round to paint the gaffer's house?' At times it was cruel, but it certainly helped break me in and to get to know the boys.

The manager's injury list then started to clear up and I found myself out of the team for a few weeks. That allowed me to work hard on my fitness. The next game I played was against St Mirren. I started the match. I had a decent game and once again ran myself into the ground. I remember Allan Preston swung in a cross, and I managed to get in front of my marker and got my head on it. I managed to beat the keeper, but the ball came off the post and a defender booted it clear. I remember for about sixty seconds after that I thought to myself, 'Wow, I've just hit the post in a professional football match.' I was still living in this little dream until the screaming started coming from the away bench. 'Get your f***in' arse back!'

Once again I was struggling for fitness come the final stages of the game. A ball then got launched down the wing and I chased after it. I don't know how I caught it, but I did, then I shaped to cross, cut back to my left and swung in a good cross for Peter Davenport to score with a diving header. I stood there in a daze again. I don't even think I went to celebrate. I had to pinch myself. It was like I was in a dream and I was just waiting for the alarm clock to go off to wake me up. I got substituted with five minutes to go, and I hardly had enough energy to drag myself off the pitch. The match ended 2–2. The atmosphere in the dressing room that weekend was a lot better. The manager praised us all, and I thought, 'Maybe I can handle this after all.'

I felt on cloud nine as I walked out of the stadium. I had played reasonably well and I felt I could make an impact in the professional ranks. I got the Man of the Match award in most of the newspapers the following day. I have to say, that gave me a bit of a buzz. I think I ended up buying just about every paper that weekend. My mum and dad still have most of the cuttings in their scrapbooks.

Paul Sturrock was absolutely amazing to me. He was fantastic and helped me make the transition to full-time football with relative ease. The manager was also really nice to my mum and dad. I appreciated that he put himself out to make my family and me feel so at home at McDiarmid Park. He was also brutally honest with me, along with John Blackley. I had never done a pre-season, and I was given extra running every day to try and get my fitness up to the rest of the lads. John, in particular, was never one to mince his words, especially out on the training pitch. I remember he used to shake his head and laugh when he got me to head the ball. I was so bad in the air that he went and got this special pole with a hook on it put up and then he hung a ball from it so I could practise my heading. It was meant to help improve my timing in the air, but most of the time it turned into a comedy sketch. The ball would be five yards in front of me when I was trying to jump up and header it. John didn't find it as funny. He said, 'You might be over six foot, but you are an absolute disgrace in the air. You are the worst header of a ball I have seen in all my time in professional football. I have never seen anybody jump for a ball and still be lower than their standing height.' I was that bad that he used to call me the 'six-foot three-inch dwarf'.

I knew that whenever Paul and John were critical that it was for my own benefit. They weren't doing it to be cruel, they were doing it to try and make me a better player. I recall the manager pulled me in and told me I had a great chance to make a real name for myself. He said I had so much skill, and already there were a number of big clubs starting to take an interest. He told me I had so much natural ability, I was so quick and I was also such a natural finisher. He used to call me 'the slewer' because I never hit the ball hard. I used to slew balls in, free-kicks and corners, with my left or right foot. He told me if I maintained the same consistency and kept listening and working hard, then I would have a real chance.

That first season was amazing. I played really well. I really enjoyed my football and I ended up winning one of the main supporters' club Player of the Year awards, although I hadn't even been at St Johnstone for the whole season. I was linked with a few top clubs like Everton, Aston Villa and Leeds United and some of the papers even compared me to Duncan Ferguson, although I think that was more down to the fact we were tall centre-forwards as we had somewhat differing styles.

As time went on and I moved out to the wing, I started to be talked about in the same way as the former Derby and Rangers winger Ted McMinn. That comparison was made at every club I played, which is not too shabby.

6

ANYTHING BUT A SAINT

My football may have been going well, but it wasn't all the land of milk and honey at St Johnstone. I was now earning decent money and the bonuses at McDiarmid Park were also terrific. The Saints' bonuses were probably the equivalent of my basic wage again. That meant only one thing. I now had big money, by my standards, and it was beginning to burn a hole in my pocket. I had more money and more time, and as any gambling addict will tell you, that is a recipe for disaster.

We had a good squad of players, a real mix of youth and experience. We had older guys like Allan Preston and Paul Cherry in the dressing room. They were always trying to help the younger boys out and give us a bit of advice. I got on well with Alan Morgan and some of the other younger boys, like Danny Griffin, Callum Davidson, Phil Scott, Stephen Robertson, Kenny Munro and Marc McCulloch. The more experienced boys would bring people in to give us financial advice and to talk about pensions and ISAs. They were trying to help us get sorted for a life outside of football, knowing that a playing career doesn't last forever. I remember just sitting there thinking, 'Why do I have to sit and listen to this tripe? All I want to do is go to the bookies or go and play golf, snooker or cards.' Basically, anything where I could win money and gamble. I wasn't interested in listening to anybody else. My future plans didn't go beyond the last horse or dog race of the day.

Thinking back to my time at McDiarmid Park, I was lucky to meet so many good and kind people. I have to say I didn't appreciate how lucky I was. Aggie Moffat and her husband, Bob, were fantastic. Aggie was like a gran to all the players at St Johnstone. She looked after us all and did everything at the club from the strips to getting everything sorted behind the scenes. Aggie and Bob looked after me a lot, which was great as a youngster coming into the football club for the first time. As I said, Paul Sturrock and John Blackley were also brilliant for me. We also had some really good players and boys at the club. If I am being honest, I knew Peter Davenport had played for Manchester United but I didn't know until after I had signed for St Johnstone just what he had achieved in the game. It is only probably now that I have grown up and matured that I realise what a quality player Peter was. I was definitely in awe of him when I first arrived, but that quickly evaporated as I got my priorities all wrong. Instead of being a full-time footballer I was probably more like a professional gambler. Bookies, bandits, pool halls or golf courses, it didn't matter to me as long as I had money on something or somebody. It is quite embarrassing because if somebody asked me now who was the most high-profile player you have played with, it would probably be Peter Davenport or Andy Goram. They were both world-class players. Peter, especially at St Johnstone, was a top striker. Everybody looked up to him. He was a very experienced player by that point and Allan Preston used to call him 'the Old Man'. I probably never gave Peter the respect he deserved, although if I am being totally truthful, I never gave anybody at St Johnstone that respect.

Allan 'Biscuits' Preston or Roddy Grant used to drive me up to Perth every day from Edinburgh. I hardly gave them a penny towards their petrol. Maybe when I had been on a winning run I would give them some money now and then, but that was pretty infrequent. My attitude to them and the rest of my team-mates was abysmal. I would think to myself, 'Why do I need to give you money? You're coming up here anyway, and you are passing my door to get here, so how am I putting you out?' That was my attitude in life.

Then one day my travelling party decided to teach me a lesson. They told me that unless I gave Roddy some money towards his petrol then they were no longer willing to pick me up. I didn't have any money to give them that particular week because I had already gambled it away. So the next morning I had to get up at the crack of dawn to get two buses to Perth. I remember I was on the bus as we came over the Forth Road Bridge. Roddy and the boys passed me in the car. They were peeping the horn, waving and laughing at me as they passed me on the bus. I took the hint, and I started to give them more petrol money but even that was never on a regular basis. I never knew what I was going to have left from one week to the next. It all depended on how my form at the bookies had been over the course of the previous two or three days.

I can now see it from their point of view. If I had been in their position, I would have done exactly the same thing. They were only trying to help me, and my attitude was 'stuff you'. They used to go out of their way to drop me closer to my house. I was so selfish and self-obsessed that I used to moan at Allan when he dropped me in Gilmerton. It was only two minutes away from Danderhall but I still moaned like anything to him. I used to say to him, 'Why can't you just drop me off in Danderhall? It's only two minutes away.' I was so lazy and ungrateful. He was taking me all the way from Edinburgh to Perth and back and I would complain because I would have to walk a mile or so down the road.

Looking back, 'Biscuits' was absolutely brilliant to me, but I couldn't see it at the time. I used to think to myself he was a bit of an idiot. This was the same guy who would chauffeur me halfway around the country. Looking back now, Allan has obviously been a very sensible guy and done well for himself, even after he had hung up the boots. He is a top football agent and a much-respected radio pundit now. And with hindsight, the only idiot around was me. I was the clown and the waste of space. The rest of the boys always had money and I never used to have a button left to my name.

It was not as if there was a gambling culture at St Johnstone. Out of all the clubs I have been at, I wouldn't say there was a lot of boys at McDiarmid Park who did a lot of betting. I was the one and only maniac at the club. I would go and do my training and then head back to Edinburgh and make for the bookies. I was a full-time footballer but there were times in the early weeks where I would go out and do some painting in the afternoon just so I could get some extra money to put on even bigger bets. I was meant to rest up between my games and training sessions, but I was either painting or punting. After a few weeks I was getting win bonuses and appearance money so I stopped the painting, especially when I was walking away with bonuses of £400 to £500 a win.

I would bet on anything, even our own games, even though we weren't meant to. To be fair, I never once bet against St Johnstone. I never had money on any of our opponents. I had a problem, but I wasn't quite in that deep at that stage.

I remember a game where we played Stenhousemuir in the Scottish Cup at Ochilview. It was on 7 February 1995. That match still sends a shiver down my spine. We had drawn 0–0 in the first game at McDiarmid. I had been up against their full-back, Euan Donaldson. I don't think I have ever given anybody a harder time on a football park in all my life. I ran him all over the shop and must have left him absolutely demented at the end of that ninety minutes. We absolutely battered them, and I couldn't believe we hadn't beaten them. It ended up going to a replay. I was supremely confident that we would go to Ochilview and run right over the top of them. As I said, in that first match we had absolutely battered Stenhousemuir, they hardly got out of their own half. I thought we were odds-on, a stick-on, a dead-cert to beat them in the replay.

I went into the bookies and we were 6/4 to win the game. I thought, 'Wow, what a price! There is no way Stenhousemuir are going to beat us.' I thought we were certainties to win – as far as I was concerned, the match was already won. We only had to turn up. I thought, 'This is unbelievable, what a chance to make some really easy money.' I ended up borrowing and stealing so much money so I could lump it on us to win the replay. I managed to scrape together £12,000 to put on us to win that day. I thought we were a dead-cert. But as every gambler knows, there is no such thing as a dead-cert.

After fifteen minutes we were 3–0 down. I remember I was taking centre with the Northern Irish international George O'Boyle, and he said to me, 'Are you okay? You look absolutely ill. You look like death warmed up.' I was chalk white, and I felt absolutely sick inside. It wasn't the fact we were being embarrassed by a lower-league club. No, I was ill because I was thinking about how much I had lost on what I thought was a so-called dead-cert. We ended up getting thumped 4–0. I lost the lot – thousands of pounds that weren't mine in the first place!

The aftermath of that game actually turned into something of a blur. We went back into the dressing room and Paul Sturrock and John Blackley went through every single one of us. John went round the team one by one, and I knew my time was coming. By the time he got to me I wasn't really that bothered about the football. John said something like, 'How can you go from being a world-beater with so many clubs looking at you, like you were on Saturday, to the one who went out there tonight and did absolutely nothing? I thought you were a completely different player. How can you be so inconsistent in back-to-back games?' There were also a fair few expletives thrown in for good measure. Getting screamed at from the management was the least of my worries. I was thinking more of all the money I had lost and how was I going to pay it back. That was an early sign of how my career was blighted by gambling.

I can also remember when I was at St Johnstone and I asked all my mates – including my cousin, Kenny Wilson – to come along and watch me play. I took money off them knowing fine they were never getting their day out. I used to take £50 a head off the boys and I would tell them to come through to Perth and they would get a day out, watch the game and get the entire works, the complete corporate experience. There were maybe twenty to twenty-five people and at £50 a head, that was a lot of money.

The boys paid me the money in good faith, but I kept cancelling or pulling the plug on their big day. I would use every excuse under the sun – like I was injured, the corporate facilities had been double-booked or I wasn't playing, even though by three in the afternoon I would be out on the pitch. I was telling all sorts of lies. Things became that bad that St Johnstone got wind of my shenanigans. The then chief executive, Stewart Duff, came up to me and said he had just had a guy on the phone saying that I had organised a corporate day out. I totally denied it. I lied right to his face. Stewart then said the guy had told him that there were twenty to twenty-five boys who had all paid me for a corporate day out at St Johnstone. These same guys were my friends, but I still couldn't see what I was doing wrong.

Eventually, I had to hold my hands up and come clean over the whole sorry scam. The boys all ended up getting their money back, but I don't think I even paid them out of my own pocket. My family or St Johnstone came to my rescue and paid the money. I didn't even have the decency to pay them back, not a penny. My cousin was so annoyed with me that he came up and gave me a bit of a doing because I had mucked so many people about. He threw a few punches at me. I don't think he wanted to do it, but he did. I think he just wanted to teach me a lesson. Where I would maybe see sense, learn from my mistakes and clean up my act. Did it make an iota of difference? No, not one.

It was hardly a surprise that my antics started to have a negative impact on my football. The second season I moved out to the wing. I always wanted to play as a winger, but I never really hit the same heights as that first season, even though I scored a few goals, including a double at Dumbarton. There was still a bit of interest in me, although I suffered a bad ankle injury that curtailed that campaign. The club told me not long after I had suffered the injury that the likes of Everton and Sheffield United were coming up to watch me. We played Clydebank and I was up against their big no-nonsense defender Kenny Brannigan. I was injured and I should never have played the match. I knew we needed to win the game because we were also still in the promotion hunt, so I played but I didn't do myself justice. I showed a bit of pace but I let myself down. Looking back, that was a big regret. I should never have played. My ankle was in bits and when I took to the field I had to strap it heavily just to get through the match.

I was out of contract at the end of that season. St Johnstone had made a good offer to re-sign, but Raith Rovers also made an offer. I should have stayed at McDiarmid Park. I knew that at the time, but I was too pig-headed. Paul Sturrock offered me more money than I was on, but it wasn't as much as I was wanting. I knew I could get what I wanted by going to Raith Rovers. I kept telling people, 'How can I knock back the chance to play in the Premier League? I might not get another opportunity. If I stay here I could end up getting a bad injury.' All my teammates at St Johnstone, from Jim Weir to Kevin McGowne, said to me, 'What are you thinking about, going to Raith Rovers? What do you want to go there for?'

I wasn't interested in listening to their views or advice. I had made up my mind. I was going to Kirkcaldy. I was getting a big signing-on fee. It was easy money, that was all that mattered to me. It wasn't about what was best for my football career. It was all about the money so I could go and blow it all in the bookies and maybe clear some of the debt I had built up over my final few months at McDiarmid Park.

When I left St Johnstone to go to Raith Rovers, I knew I was making a mistake. St Johnstone were still in the First Division, while Raith, under Jimmy Nicholl, had just won the Coca-Cola Cup and had survived their first season in the Scottish Premier Division. I was moving up to the top flight, but I didn't think for a minute that we were going to survive. I was also more than aware that there would be a fair chance that St Johnstone could pass us on the way down. Saints hadn't been far away the previous season, so they were always going to be there or thereabouts in the First Division promotion race the next year. But the real deciding factor was getting my hands on the money.

7

A RAITH ROLE MODEL AND GREETINGS FROM GAZZA

I moved to Kirkcaldy, desperate to do well for Raith Rovers and to show I was good enough to play at the top level. If you look at my journey to the Scottish Premier Division, it was a rapid rise. Two years earlier, I had been playing local amateur football in Edinburgh and working as a painter. Now I was suddenly in the top flight of Scottish football, on the same pitches as top stars like Paul Gascoigne, Brian Laudrup, Paolo Di Canio and Jorge Cadete. It was a script that wouldn't have looked out of place in Roy of the Rovers, never mind Raith Rovers. I had come from nowhere to rubbing shoulders with Scotland's elite.

I knew it was going to be hard. Raith had survived their first season in the top flight but there had been a lot of change from the team who had famously beaten Celtic to lift the Coca-Cola Cup. That side, under the guidance of the legendary Jimmy Nicholl, will go down as one of the greatest in the club's history, and quite rightly so. As everyone knows, success in football comes at a cost, and it certainly did at Rovers. Nicholl was head-hunted by English side Millwall, and he took several of his key players with him, like Stevie Crawford, Jason Dair and Davie Sinclair. Other top stars from that side were also sold for big money, as Raith accepted a club-record bid from Bolton for Steve

McAnespie and another half-decent offer from Hearts for Colin Cameron. It really was the end of an era.

The Raith board had turned to their former player Jimmy Thomson to replace Nicholl. Jimmy had been in charge of Dunfermline, Alloa Athletic and Berwick Rangers and already had a fair bit of managerial experience. The problem for Jimmy was that he was facing up to an almost impossible task. Nicholl had worked minor miracles at Starks Park, and whoever replaced him was always going to be judged by previous achievements. It probably could have been classed as Mission Impossible because I am not sure even Sir Alex Ferguson or José Mourinho could have maintained the level of success that the Coca-Cola Cup-winning team had. It was a real golden generation for Raith Rovers. It is one that is unlikely to be repeated, although I hope for the sake of the fans and the club that the good times do return to Kirkcaldy. The Rovers support have had a rough ride since then, and they deserve a bit of success because they are a loyal, loyal set of fans.

Jimmy Thomson was from Edinburgh, and I first heard through the grapevine that he was keen to sign me from St Johnstone. He then phoned and explained how he was building a new team and believed I could be a big part of it. As I have said, the lure of playing in the Scottish Premier Division was a big thing, although I knew if I had stayed at St Johnstone then I probably would have got that chance sooner rather than later. I also wanted the money and I make no secret of that. The signing-on fee allowed me to pay off some of my gambling debts, like bank loans that I had managed to pile up while in Perth. I was also getting more money every week and the bonuses were good, so I knew I would have more to gamble away. So I probably went to Raith more from a gambling point of view than anything else.

When Jimmy came in there were still a few survivors from the Coca-Cola Cup-winning team. Goalkeeper Scott Thomson remained between the sticks, while we still had Shaun Dennis and the captain Danny Lennon. Apart from that, Jimmy was given a bit of a blank canvas to go out and build his new-look team. He brought in Paul Harvey, David Craig, Paul Browne and myself. I think Jimmy signed six or seven players that summer. I still have a cutting from one of the newspapers that shows me standing with the rest of Jimmy's new recruits.

Jimmy got a lot of criticism for some of the boys he signed. I suppose I also fell into that category. The critics were saying that the players were all coming from the lower leagues and weren't established in the top flight. I suppose, when you look at it, they were probably right. I was making the move from St Johnstone and I had never played anywhere other than the First Division, and it was a bit of a gamble. What I would say in Jimmy's defence was that he signed players who had the potential to do well. Paul Browne was a defender who arrived from Aston Villa, and he came up highly recommended by the legendary former Manchester United defender Paul McGrath. We also had some decent players like Scott 'Nipper' Thomson, Peter Duffield, John Millar, Tony Rougier, Jim McInally and Davie Kirkwood. We should have done a lot better than we did, but we never really gelled as a team. We never got going at all, although also in fairness to Jimmy, he was given a bit of a baptism of fire. His first two league games of the 1996–97 season saw us open up with away games to Rangers and Celtic. Immediately that left us with a mountain to climb and well short of confidence.

We went to Ibrox and Jimmy told us he wanted all his players behind the ball. We did reasonably well, although we lost 1–0. Trevor Steven scored the only goal of the game midway through the first half. Jimmy came in after the game. We used to call him

'Slippers' because he always had them on, even at the big grounds like Ibrox and Celtic Park. He very rarely wore shoes. We had done okay, we had contained Rangers without ever looking like we were going to do anything against them. Jimmy told us we had made a great start. He also insisted that when it came to the other teams, it would be a lot easier because Rangers were the best team in Scotland at that point.

That was my first appearance at Ibrox, and I think I was a bit overwhelmed by the occasion. I don't know what it was about playing at Rangers because I didn't have that many good games there. I went and played well at Parkhead, but very rarely did I produce the goods at Ibrox. I put that down to the electronic scoreboards there. They used to put up the half-time results and it wouldn't be the first time at Ibrox that I would be paying more attention to the scoreboard than the game. The play would be racing past me and I would be too busy trying to see what the other scores were and whether my coupon was up or down.

It was hardly a surprise that I struggled to cope with my enhanced wage packet. My gambling was beginning to spiral out of control. I was getting more and more money, and that meant even more bets. More stupid and bigger bets. I was betting beyond my means, and I was starting to have real issues. I was hardly the ideal man you would be looking for to dig you out when you were in trouble, which is what Jimmy Thomson was looking for because he and the team were really struggling.

Jimmy went with the same approach he had adopted at Ibrox and took it to Parkhead, but it didn't have the same impact. We got thumped 4–1. When I look back now, I just wish Jimmy had been a bit more adventurous as we had good attacking players. Getting forward was certainly my forte. I couldn't defend for toffee, so I just wish he had opened up and given some of the boys the chance to have a go and show people what we could do. When we went to places like Ibrox and Parkhead, we were just going there to get thumped. We never gave ourselves a chance, at least when I went back to grounds like that with Motherwell I felt we had a wee bit of a chance.

It was around that time that Jimmy decided to step down. He thought it was better for the club if they went in another direction. I was genuinely saddened and upset when he left. Jimmy had given me my chance in the top flight, and I also knew he had put his heart and soul into the Raith job. He is also a really nice guy and has a lovely family. People argued that he wasn't up to managing in the Scottish Premier Division. What I would say is that Jimmy had the club and everybody at it in his heart. He genuinely cared for Raith Rovers and wanted the best for them. I know he was hurting as much as anybody when we hit the bottom of the league. I still see Jimmy and his family in Edinburgh, and he always has time for me. We always speak about Raith because we had some good times there, even though the results didn't go as well as either of us had hoped.

Raith turned to the former Motherwell and Hearts boss, Tommy McLean. He was an experienced and proven manager at the top level. I thought we could really progress under him. I also knew he was a bit of a disciplinarian, so I also secretly hoped that he could maybe get a hold of me, getting me focused on football rather than gambling. Unfortunately, Tommy was hardly there long enough to remember many of our names, never mind get his feet under the desk. He took charge for one game, a 4–1 home defeat to Aberdeen, and then resigned days later to become the new manager at Dundee United, where his brother Jim was the chairman.

That left us on the lookout for another new manager and this time it was another experienced campaigner in Iain Munro that came in. He had a proven track record. He could name

Dunfermline, St Mirren and Hamilton on his managerial curriculum vitae. That period, however, summed up the uncertainty at the club because Rovers ended up having four managers in the space of a fourteen-month period. The job was going to be an almighty one for him or anybody else for that matter. I knew four or five league games into my Rovers career that we were going to struggle, and I had made a massive mistake leaving St Johnstone. We gave it a go, but we were pretty much the whipping boys in the league. I think we all knew by the Christmas that we were going down. It was hard because we spent most of our time on the back foot. We had good players but our confidence had taken a battering and there was an air of inevitability about the place.

Iain came in and helped us stage a mini-revival. I managed to net the winner in a 3–2 win over Dundee United, while we also drew with Hearts and Rangers. I scored in that game against Rangers at a time when the champions had top, top players. That was at the time when Rangers were spending big money on some of the biggest stars in Europe, like Paul Gascoigne. The England star very rarely used to do his warm-up out on the pitch. He used to go to the gym and do his own little workout. So that day I saw him go into the little gym we had a Starks Park. It was beside the physio's room. I threw on my gear and I thought, 'I have to go in there – it's Gazza.' I never used to go into the gym before games but that day I couldn't get my trainers on quick enough. You have to remember, this was only my third season as a professional footballer and to me he was like football royalty.

I told the physio I wanted to warm my legs up but I only went into the room to see Gazza. I sat on the bike next to him and we started talking. It was so unreal – this was somebody who I had absolutely idolised as a footballer. He was so genuine, and what a nice person. He might have been a multi-million-aire and one of the biggest celebrities in the country but he was just so grounded. He wasn't big-time at all. He was so open and when we were on the bikes he started talking about his life, his time with his wife Cheryl and how difficult it was for him up in Scotland with photographers and the press following him around constantly. I was just about to leave the room when I turned and said, 'Thank you. It has been really good to chat to you because you are one of my heroes. I'm just delighted to have had the chance to speak to you and I really hope everything works out for you up here because you have been absolutely brilliant for Scottish football.' I then walked out. We acknowledged each other on the pitch and that was that.

My day had already been made by the fact that I got to speak to Gazza. I didn't think things could get any better, but they did. The match was still goalless when my Raith teammate Tony Rougier ran into the Rangers goalkeeper Theo Snelders. Snelders was left stranded in no man's land in the middle of the Rangers half. I was standing at the side, and the ball just broke to me. I was thirty yards out with an open goal. I fired it into the empty net and put Raith 1–0 up. I hardly got a chance to celebrate when our defender Shaun Dennis jumped on top of me. As a big Celtic fan, I think he was even happier than me. I eventually managed to escape from Shaun's grasp and as I walked back to the halfway line somebody shouted, 'Hoy.' I looked around but I had no idea who it was. I then turned again and Gazza was standing there with a smirk on his face. He said, 'I would never have spoken to you if I knew you were going to do something like that.' I laughed my head off so much. The match ended up 2–2, and Gazza and I had a good laugh and joke about things after the game. That is a day I will never forget from my time in football.

Another evening I got to mix it with Europe's elite came in January 1997, when Bayern Munich came back for the opening of the newly developed Starks Park. Unfortunately, unlike their last visit, in the UEFA Cup, it wasn't for a competitive fixture. I recall the game. It was good to play against some of the best players in the world. I actually won a penalty when Thomas Helmer brought me down inside the box. I was left raging because I wanted to take the spot kick but the captain, Danny Lennon, grabbed the ball off me and then missed it. The only football shirt I have from my time in football is Markus Munch's Bayern Munich top from that game. I got Markus, Helmer and Jürgen Klinsmann to sign the jersey, and I still have it framed and up in the house.

By that time, we knew we were all but relegated. We were at the bottom end of the table and survival was slipping further and further away with every morale-sapping defeat. We finished rock bottom of the top ten. We were thirteen points behind second-last Hibs, so that showed how much we had struggled. I think it is fair to say it was a campaign we were all glad to see the back of. The summer break couldn't come quickly enough for us. I thought after my first season that I had done enough to get another move. There was a bit of speculation and interest, but nothing came of it. I went back to Raith, but it was hard for everybody to lift ourselves after the relegation. It is fair to say there was a bit of hangover in and around the club for several months after we dropped down into the First Division.

Things didn't work out the way I had hoped football-wise at Raith, but I still have a lot of friends from my time there, like Craig Dargo and Keith Wright. All the boys at Rovers used to call us the 'Three Amigos' because we all came through from Edinburgh and hung about together. Keith joined Raith in my second season when we were in the First Division. Everyone thought it was strange that Keith and I got on so well together because he was such a big Hibee and I was a Jambo, but we managed to overcome our obvious differences to become good friends. Keith was also an experienced player at that stage of my career. He has played for Dundee and won the Skol Cup with Hibs, so he was good to have around. He had the experience, and he was like a mentor for me at that stage.

'Dargs' was one of the youngsters at the club when I was at Rovers. He was from Edinburgh and he started to give me a lift through to Kirkcaldy after Jimmy had left because I couldn't drive. He used to take me to training and back and basically wherever else I wanted to go. We spent a lot of time together and from that we formed a really close friendship. I used to get Dargs to drop me off at one of the bookies on Minto Street in Edinburgh. I used to leave him with the car running outside. I would tell him I would be five minutes and forty-five minutes later he would still be sitting there, beeping his horn and absolutely fuming with me. He should have driven off and left me, but I don't think he ever did. He eventually started to come into the bookies with me. He has since admitted he was in his element watching me punt. Even now he says that he used to look up to me. I was a player Rovers had paid a wee bit of money for, I was earning a decent wage and I was starting to come out of my shell. I was also one of the more vocal characters in the Starks Park dressing room. I was no longer the timid, young boy who was scared to say boo to a goose like when I had first arrived at St Johnstone. Dargs claimed he wanted to get to that level where, like me, he would be an established first-team player. It is embarrassing when I look back. How could anybody have looked up to me? Everything may have looked good and well on the outside, but inside I was a very different person who, through gambling, was raging a one-man war to hurt myself and everybody close to me.

49

Dargs was the trainee and I was the full-time professional, but there were times where I was having to borrow money off him so I could get my bets on. We used to have a laugh and a joke when we were in the bookies. I would say, 'I have got a bet on this horse or dog race, see if you can guess what one it is.' He would come back and say, 'It is the favourite, dog two, at 3–1, etc.' I would then say, 'How did you know?' We would then watch the race. Dargs said that I always used to bite my nails when I watched the races. I don't know if it is a nervous reaction or not. We would watch the television and my dog would be leading the race all the way but would come up short in the final straight and finish second or third. Dargs would always joke I should have bet it each-way. I would then pull my betting slip out of my pocket and it would have the winner's number on it. I did that a few times, although there were also a good few occasions where my dog or horse didn't come in. That is the thing when you have a gambling problem, you try and keep everything a secret. You try and hide your bets and the only people who know what you are doing are the cashier and yourself.

Also when we used to go on nights out we would end up at the casino in Newington. Dargs would come with me. I would cash in hundreds of pounds of chips, sometimes my entire week's wage. I was on a basic of £900 a week before bonuses and appearance money. Even Dargs laughs about things now. He would cash £10 and still have it most of the night and my stash would be gone in a flash, basically minutes, and I was back at the desk cashing even more money. I must have been a croupier's dream, throwing good money after bad. I was really starting to get out of control and bet money that I didn't have. Dargs jokes that he only went to the casino to keep me company and to get something to eat, like a toasted sandwich at the end of the night. I only had an appetite for destruction.

I borrowed so much money off Dargs and never paid him back. He was only a kid at the time, and even when he moved on to Kilmarnock I was still taking money off him. I would make up some sob story and he would be there at the drop of a hat to give me the cash. I was making really good money at Motherwell but he had to wait ages and ages to get what he was owed. I was just throwing the money away at the bookies or the casino.

I have dragged so many good people down with my gambling. I am just glad Dargs wasn't one of them. Dargs was one of the first people I told when I decided I needed help and it wasn't until I told him that he realised how bad my problem was. When you have a gambling problem, you try to keep your betting a secret from everybody else. It is a sort of defence mechanism. To be fair to Dargs, he has been fantastic and been really supportive of me. Eventually, when I was able to sort my life out, I was able to pay him back every penny he had loaned me. I am just glad I still have him as a friend. He is so loyal and my best friend. That was why he was the best man at my wedding, along with Elliott Smith, who was a young boy at Hearts when I was there. I know just about everything about Dargs and his family, and he knows all about me and mine. We are really close. He is like the little brother I never had. He is a fantastic boy and I look up to him so much. He has his own family now and Jac is really close to his fiancée Dawn and his son Kyle. We go away on holidays together and we speak to each other all the time. They are a lovely, lovely family. He is a model dad, husband and son. His family mean the world to him.

Maybe I should have been a bit more like Dargs. He has his head screwed on right. He has had a very good football career and has property and invested his money well away from the game. He has done well at every club he has been at, from Raith,

Kilmarnock, Inverness Caledonian Thistle, St Mirren, Dumbarton and Partick Thistle. The fans at every club he has been at speak of him really fondly. That shows what a good player he is. I am actually surprised he never got a bigger move because he certainly had the ability to play for a big club in Scotland or England.

I know I owe him a lot more than he owes me. That is why I try to look after Dargs and help him and his family whenever I can. I know it is the least I can do. He looked up to me during his football career and he has learned a lot from me. Some good things and a lot of bad things. He knows my football career should have been a lot better, and I think he has learned from that and hopefully that has helped him avoid the pitfalls that led to my downfall. His friendship is the one thing that I will take from my time at Raith.

I am just sorry that there weren't more good times on the pitch at Raith Rovers. The second season I did my ankle and by the time I got fit, a £125,000 bid for me had come in from Morton. Raith needed the money after the relegation from the top flight, and so I decided to move. It was a deal that suited all parties. I certainly have a lot of good memories from my time at Rovers and I still have a lot of friends there too. I still get on well with Ally Gourlay, who helps with the match programme and does a lot of stuff for the club.

I have gone back to Raith quite a few times in recent years and I have made a couple of the half-time draws. I have always got a really good reception from the fans. I must have done something right when I was there. I just wish I could have done a bit more and could have brought a bit more success to their club.

8

BLOWING A TON AT CAPPIELOW

My gambling shaped my career. I went to Morton because I was being offered decent money. I got another signing-on fee and that allowed me to pay off the debts I had left over from my time at Raith Rovers. When I moved it always allowed me to temporarily get out of the vicious circle of debt I was in. I would repay my loans and give most of the money back I had borrowed, mainly from my mum or Auntie Margaret. I also saw moving to Greenock as a big thing for me at that stage of my life. It was a way of wiping the slate clean. I could start afresh and maybe try and clean up my act a bit. The priority, however, was getting that first signing-on fee. I think I got roughly £30,000 when I signed on at Morton. The club offered to pay it over three instalments, which would have been better for me because I wouldn't have had to pay so much tax, but I wasn't interested. I was just desperate to get my hands on the money. The quicker I could get the money the better. I also knew Morton were desperate to get me, and that allowed me to play hardball until I got what I was looking for. I refused to budge until they agreed to pay my signing-on fee in two instalments, even though it would cost me more in tax. I didn't care. I needed the money. I wanted the money. I had the tills of the local William Hill, Ladbrokes or Coral's to fill. I could clear my feet and then think about starting all over again.

People in Edinburgh, in my regular bookies, knew I was a mad gambler, and I also started to get a bit of a reputation in Kirkcaldy amongst the locals and my Raith teammates. I thought going to Greenock would be good because it was far enough out of the way. Nobody knew me or knew I had a problem. I believed I could go into bookies in Greenock and Port Glasgow without people coming up to pester or talk to me. I wanted to be Mr Anonymous. I hated people knowing what I was doing. Gambling made me absolutely paranoid. In saying that, at Raith, my gambling had still been under reasonable control by my standards. I had always bet everything I had earned and maybe had a few loans, but my debts were still manageable – even though I never had a penny left in my pocket.

Morton were in the First Division as well but they were doing well, and I felt they were better equipped to try and win promotion than Raith Rovers. I just felt Raith were perhaps on a downward spiral. I thought Morton probably had a better team and another big pull in my decision was the manager Billy Stark. He was a big player and a big name. He was a massive star for Aberdeen and Celtic. He had that successful spell at Pittodrie when I was growing up as a kid under Sir Alex Ferguson. I went and met Billy, and he was very ambitious. He wanted to lead the team into the Scottish Premier League and I also felt he would be a good manager to play under. I genuinely believed that Morton could go and challenge for promotion.

The team also had some good players like Owen Archdeacon, who is a great lad, John Anderson, Warren Hawke and my old St Johnstone teammate Harry Curran. I went there and I fitted in really well. It helped that we had a good team, a good bunch of boys, and the fans were brilliant as well.

I was also getting decent money by First Division standards. I think I got about £1,000 a week basic, with appearance and bonus money on top. It was a good set-up at Cappielow, although it was fair to say that not everything was so rosy behind the scenes. I got on well with the supporters, but they certainly didn't share the same love with our chairman Hugh Scott. The fans were unhappy with some aspects of how the club was being run. I have to say it didn't really affect the players too much. There were a couple of occasions where our wages were late, but we always got the money we were due in the end.

On the football side of things, Billy Stark and his assistant manager Frank Connor did a great job keeping us solely focused on the games. I got on amazingly well with Frank. I think if I hadn't been totally dragged down by gambling then Frank and Billy could really have pushed my football career on. I don't think either of them had any idea of my gambling or how bad it really was. Frank was very supportive to me and always had words of encouragement. I remember Billy and Frank pulled me into their office one afternoon. They were trying to get more out of me and to make me more consistent. I was a stereotypical winger who blew hot and cold one week to the next. Frank had been a coach at Celtic, and he told me that he had never seen somebody with so much ability but who could be so infuriating as well. Have you heard that somewhere before? That was something that was laid at my door throughout my career. I would either be good or bad.

Frank and Billy both had strong connections with Celtic. They told me that Celtic had been interested in signing me when I had been at St Johnstone, but it didn't happen because of politics. I was never aware of their interest or even the fact they had been watching me. I also didn't know what they meant when they said politics, although I never actually asked them. I don't know if there really had been an interest from Celtic or if it was just their way of trying to build up my self-confidence. Regardless,

I remember walking out of the manager's office feeling like I was on top of the world.

I really enjoyed playing under Billy and Frank. Billy is still in the game and is doing a great job with the Scotland Under-21 team. He is still helping people along the way. The amazing thing about Billy and Frank was that they were complete polar opposites. They were like chalk and cheese. Billy was so laid-back and calm, but when Frank exploded you knew you would be facing a volcanic eruption.

I remember there was a match against Partick Thistle we lost. Billy came in and never lost the plot. You could sense when he was annoyed and angry, but that was very rare. Billy was such a placid and laid-back person. He came in and told us we hadn't been good enough and we were too up and down, but not to worry about it because it was all about bouncing back the next week. It was all about getting the chins up again and then he walked out the dressing room. It was funny because Billy had just stepped outside when Frank came in and started screaming and shouting at everyone. He turned the air blue and everybody got it, regardless of whether they had been good, bad or indifferent. He went mental, and when Frank lost it, he *really* lost it! Frank was hard but fair. I like that in people. I also liked his honesty and the way he got to the point. He didn't beat around the bush. I had so much respect for him because you always knew where you stood with Frank. He was also a very good coach, and if there was one person I could have chosen to mentor me through my career then it would definitely have been him. He was an amazing person. If he had been there to watch my every move, then I am in no doubt I could have made so much more of my career.

I remember there was one game when we played Celtic in the Scottish Cup at Cappielow. It was live on Sky Television and was quite a big occasion for the club. It was one of Mark Viduka's first games, and they beat us 3–0. The big Australian international scored a double, and Henrik Larsson also netted that night. It sounds like we got a bit of a chasing but we actually did quite well. I did okay, and I was pleased when I walked off at the end. Frank came in and said he was amazed that I hadn't been named as the Man of the Match. It went to Paul Fenwick – known as Big Paul, who was a Canadian international footballer and later moved on to Hibs – but I didn't really have too many complaints because the big man did really well that night against two world-class centre-forwards.

The second season I was joined at Morton by one of my old Raith Rovers teammates, Keith Wright. I spent a lot of time with Keith during our time together at Morton. He was my partner in crime, and we'd often go to the bookies together. Keith is a very sociable guy but he also has his head screwed on the right way; he could go out and put on a few bets without going mad. He had a lot more self-discipline than me. He didn't know I was blowing all my wages because I tried to hide it, although I think he knew I had an issue, but he probably thought it was a fairly minor one.

I used to travel through to Edinburgh with Paul, Keith and Kevin Thomas. To be fair, Keith or Kevin never really moaned that I didn't give them petrol money, it was mainly Paul Fenwick. He had every right because they were taking me right back to the house. Paul was a top guy but once again I used and abused him. I hardly used to give him any petrol money. It was a bit like St Johnstone all over again, even though it was a longer journey from Edinburgh down to Greenock. This time I was on the most money out of all the boys, but I still couldn't put my hand in my pocket and help out with the fuel costs. My behaviour and attitude were totally shocking.

I have to be honest, the car journeys may have been free, but they were also killing me. I actually started to stay down on a Friday night when we had home games. It was becoming a bit of a pain driving two hours before a match. I used to come into the dressing room as stiff as a board, so I decided to go down on the Friday night if we were playing at Cappielow. I ended up staying in a local bed and breakfast where the club put up some of their players. That turned out to be a bad move. As soon as I had finished training, I was out of the ground and straight to the bookies. I would stay there and wouldn't leave until the last race was over or the bookies was about to shut. I would eventually troop back to the bed and breakfast between 6.30pm and 7pm. The landlord would always say to me, 'You are awfully late. The rest of the boys were back hours ago.' I would then tell a pack of lies that I had been doing extra training or I had been here or there. I never once told him I had been out gambling my afternoon away. On the rare occasion when I did come out on top and I had money, then I would just end up using my winnings to put on a big football coupon for the Saturday. That was on the unusual occasions when I actually had money left. Very rarely did I come home on a Friday with anything but empty pockets. If I had money left then it would have been gambled.

When I first went to Morton we used to get paid on a Friday every week. The club then changed their payday and told people that we would be getting paid monthly. That caused me serious cash-flow problems. When that happened, I was never out of the front office at Morton asking for an advance on my following month's wage. It happened a few times at St Johnstone and Raith, but it became more regular when I was on a monthly wage at Morton. The office staff at Cappielow used to laugh when they saw me coming through the door. It could only mean one thing. I was always short of money because I would blow all my wages in the first few days. In some good weeks, I would be left with something like £100 to see me through, but in most cases it was a lot less than that.

When I started to pick up my monthly wage packet I really saw how much I was starting to lose. I was gambling anything between £4,000 to £5,000 at a time, depending on the bonuses and appearance money I had picked up that month. It wasn't so bad when I was getting paid weekly, but when I got my monthly sum, it allowed me to bet big. That was when things really started to spiral out of control. I loved to bet on everything. I was the sort of punter who would have £100 on twenty races, then maybe have £2,000 on one horse.

The problem is that the more I won, the more the bookies got back. They were the only winners. I would walk out and think, 'I can't believe I had so many winners today.' I had maybe had five or six winners, but the chances were that I still had less money in my pocket because I had bet my winnings away again. I just kept going and going. I was never one to quit when I was ahead. That is just not in a gambler's nature. If I had then I might be a lot richer than I am today. I was earning good money. I should have been living comfortably, but at that point I was on my uppers.

In my real day job, well the one I was paid to do, Morton weren't doing too badly either. In the 1998–99 season, we weren't actually that far away from the promotion places, although we fell away in the final few months. Hibs, under Alex McLeish, eventually ran away with the league, some distance ahead of Falkirk, Ayr United, Airdrie, St Mirren and us. I recall we were still on the fringes of the title race going into the last couple of months. I remember I took two jags in my ankle so I could play. I ran about daft, feeling brilliant, but I ended up suffering for the next three or four days after it. I could hardly walk. That's the reason why I never took another jag in my career. I still have problems with my ankle today and I put a lot of that down to those injections.

Overall, I felt I did quite well at Morton. I also chipped in with a few goals. It helped because I took all the set pieces. A big goal for me that season was a free-kick I scored against Hibs. It is one I won't forget in a hurry. We were at Easter Road and we got a free-kick pretty close to the touchline. I knew I was hated by the Hibs fans because they used to give me dog's abuse just because I was a Jambo. I never expected anything less. There was a man in the family enclosure beside where I was taking the free-kick from. I could hear this guy shouting at me, 'I hope you die of cancer, you Hearts b******.' The play had stopped and this idiot just berated me non-stop for two or three minutes. I knew the Hibs fans hated me, but I didn't realise how much. This was coming from a family section in front of kids, but even that didn't stop him. I chose to ignore him. I knew it wasn't worth getting involved, although it was hard.

This vile torrent of abuse continued until I took the kick. I whipped it in really hard. It was a cross and the goalkeeper Oli Gottskálksson had expected somebody to get a touch, but nobody got near it and the ball flew right into the net. I turned and looked at the guy who had been abusing me. He was going off his nut at me. He was that bad the stewards had to hold him back. I just decided it was best for all concerned to leave it, and I ran back for the kick-off. Unfortunately my day was ruined when Pat McGinlay scored a late winner to give Hibs a 2–1 win. At least the Hibs fan would have gone home a bit happier.

Morton were keen to keep me beyond the end of the season. Billy Stark had sat me down and offered me terms, but I was keen to consider my options. My agent then came to me with an offer to try my luck in Norway. Lyn of Oslo offered me a two-year contract on great money. Billy knew he couldn't compete with what they had offered. I think he also thought I might have been able to take my career on by going to Scandinavia.

I went out there for a couple of weeks to see what Oslo and Norwegian football was like. Lyn played in the national stadium, the Ullevaal, at the time, which was a real footballing arena. The club also had me staying in this magnificent flat right in the main street in Oslo. It must have cost Lyn an absolute fortune. It was right in a real up-market area of the city and they were obviously out to try and impress me and to convince me to sign.

The money was really good, but the funny thing was that Lyn were only part-time. They didn't have any full-time players. Very few of the Norway's top teams were full time. They only trained three nights a week, but all the boys were still mega-fit. I played in a few games and trained with Lyn. It was good, and everybody played their part to make me feel welcome. They did everything they could to make me happy, but I decided it wasn't for me and I turned their offer down.

To be fair, Lyn were offering more money than I had ever earned in my career but I knew it wasn't for me. And one of the main reasons I couldn't settle was because I couldn't bet. There was next to no betting in Norway, so needless to say I couldn't get home quick enough. That was why I joined Motherwell. I was demented by the time I got home, and I was only in Oslo for a couple of weeks. I was bored – there was nothing for me to do. I got that bad that I was even phoning home and getting people to put bets on for me back in Scotland. I started to get withdrawal symptoms and I just didn't know what to do with myself. That was how bad things got. I now look back and I think, 'What a massive opportunity I let slip through my fingers.'

I came back to Motherwell and signed for half the money I was offered in Norway. There were also personal reasons why I didn't want to go to Norway. My niece, Kelsa, was born on 3 December 1998. She was only a few months old, and I didn't want to miss her growing up. I also missed my mum, sister and even my dad, although my relationship at that time wasn't as strong with him as it is today.

The cost of living in Norway also put me off that move. We had a night out and most of the boys didn't come out until later because they had been drinking in their homes. That wasn't for me. I wanted to be out and be the life and soul of the party. So we went out and there were six or seven of us, and I said I would buy the first round but all the other boys were telling me they would buy their own. I wouldn't let it lie and I bought them all drinks. The bar man then charged me £10 a drink for what was the equivalent of a quarter-pint of beer. I quickly realised why people don't go out early in Norway. They obviously thought I was big-time, but I never offered another round after that.

I knew within a couple of days of being in Norway that Motherwell had taken notice of me. My agent told me that Billy Davies had shown a lot of interest in me. That was also at the back of my mind when I made my decision. It was another chance to step up to the Scottish Premier League and so everything pointed to me heading back home. What would I have done if the Lyn deal was the only one on the table? Genuinely, I don't know if I would have stayed out in Norway or not. I think it would have been soul-destroying if I had been forced to stay there. That is not being disrespectful to Oslo, the club or the Norwegian people. It is a lovely place, but a lack of gambling facilities and the fact it was so far away from Scotland made it a no go. Oslo is an amazing city and I was being offered something different, but it just never appealed to me. They offered me big, big money but it wouldn't have mattered how much they offered me because it was too far from home and too far from my gambling.

9

FIR PARK FEVER

I was only home from Norway a day when I went through to talk to Motherwell. I knew they were a big club and they had invested big money into their squad over the previous couple of seasons. I went and met with Dave McParland, who was their chief scout, because the manager, Billy Davies, was away on holiday. McParland told me he had been the guy who had recommended me to the manager. He revealed he had watched me quite a lot and felt I could use Motherwell as a stepping-stone to bigger things and how he felt Billy could help get the best out of me. He told me what sort of money I would get and a bit of background about the club. I had a good vibe and Motherwell definitely appealed to me, but I wanted to speak to the manager face to face to hear his thoughts and how I fitted into his plans before I committed.

I went back and met Billy a week and a half later. As soon as I met him I realised what a genuinely nice guy he was. I also got a good feeling from him and felt I really could flourish under his management at Motherwell. He was frank and honest when he spoke. He sat me down, pointed out my flaws, what was good about my play and where I could work to improve my game. After that, my mind was made up. I felt it was the right move for me, and I signed my contract with Motherwell.

That was two or three weeks into the summer of 1999. I couldn't wait to get going. I started to do a lot of running to get myself fit and ready to hit the ground when I returned for pre-season training. A week or so before we were due to return, I started to feel really drained and washed out. I kept working out but eventually I had to give in and go and see the doctor. I was told I had glandular fever. I was totally devastated. I was warned I couldn't do anything physical and I just had to rest because it was such a debilitating illness. The doctor warned me that if I kept going then I would have made myself and my condition even worse. Not what I wanted to hear before I had even had the chance to meet my new teammates, never mind got to kick a ball in claret and amber. I had to phone Billy and explain the situation. I know it was a nightmare for him, but it was even worse for me because I was desperate to impress and to get my Motherwell career up and running.

I wasn't even allowed to have any contact with the rest of the boys because of the nature of my illness and the fact that the virus was contagious. It is such a soul-destroying illness. There is nothing you can do. It just completely floors you. I had just to stay at home and rest. I was absolutely spent. The fact that I couldn't play or train was a real blow. It put me on a real downer and probably led to an early bout of depression. It didn't help that I was still getting paid by the club and I also had been given a half-decent signing-on fee. That gave me even more money and time to gamble. I was meant to be resting, but I ended up spending most days in the bookies. I think the combination of glandular fever and gambling started to get on top of me.

I was earning more money at that point than at any other stage in my career. I was on about £1,450 a week basic, but I also would eventually pick up big appearance money, along with really good win bonuses. If I played I could earn big money by comparison with what I had been on earlier in my career. My wages were heavily weighted on appearances because Billy Davies didn't really expect me to play every week. It was very much incentive-based and it was up to me to do well. I never went to Fir Park thinking I would set the place on fire, but I was confident in my own abilities. I also certainly wasn't on the big bucks that the likes of Andy Goram and John Spencer were earning. I knew I was in a different world from them. It was all about trying to establish myself and building up from there. I was in a similar boat to Derek Townsley. He was another big winger that the club signed that summer from another lower league club in the shape of Queen of the South. We both came in hungry to do well.

I was on good money but I had no thoughts about the future. I was meant to be resting in those early weeks, but I was in the bookies gambling ridiculous amounts. I had even more money to throw away. I was suddenly losing bigger sums in less time. Between that and my physical condition, not surprisingly, I felt really low. I was so down that I seriously questioned whether I was ever going to be fit enough to play professional football again. It was about that time that things started to click inside my head – what gambling was actually doing to me, mentally and physically.

The rest of the boys had done all their pre-season and went abroad to play games. It wasn't until four weeks after I signed that I finally got to meet them. I had, however, been in constant contact with Billy on the phone, but that had been it, although the manager was great and brilliant at keeping my spirits up. The team had a friendly against Queen's Park at Hampden and that was when I was given the all-clear to go to a game for the first time.

I looked up to a lot of the boys at Motherwell. There were a lot of unbelievable names there. There was Andy Goram, John Spencer, Shaun Teale, Ged Brannan and Don Goodman. It was amazing. I was star-struck. It was like being back at St Johnstone when I signed professional forms for the first time.

When I walked into the dressing room for the first time, this little character wandered up to me and said, 'Hi, Cyrus.'

I replied, 'Cyrus?'

And he said, 'Hi, I'm John Spencer, and you must be Cyrus the Virus.'

He walked away laughing and continued to slaughter me with stuff like, 'You are meant to be here setting up chances for me and you have been lying at home in your bed. What have we been paying you for?'

I was so embarrassed being wound up in front of so many big top names. 'Spenny' then went away and turned up the music in the room and started dancing. It was like a flashback to McDiarmid Park again. I thought once again, 'How am I ever going to stand up for myself getting stick from somebody like that?' This was a top, top striker who had played for Chelsea, Queen's Park Rangers, Everton and Scotland. I thought I was quite streetwise at that point. I had been one of the main characters in the dressing rooms at Raith and Morton, but this was another level. I would always stand up for myself and I would never let anybody take the mick out of me. I always had an answer for everyone until I met Spenny. He was like the Taz – the Tazmanian Devil – because he was this bundle of non-stop energy.

I have to say I felt really intimidated as I walked round the dressing room and introduced myself to the other boys, like Goram, Brannan, Goodman, McCulloch, Tony Thomas and Steve McMillan. It was a room full of celebrities. I thought at that point, 'I have finally arrived.' I had played in the Scottish Premier

League before with Raith, but this was different. I don't mean to sound disrespectful to any of my previous teammates, but I felt my football career was really starting. I was now in a team who had players who were massive in the game.

I actually had to wait another two or three weeks after that before I could start training. I was still being monitored closely by the doctor to make sure I was fit enough to go back into full-time training. It felt like forever, especially as I was spending all my time and money in the bookies. I was desperate to start playing because I wanted to make an impression at Fir Park and I was also probably looking for an excuse to get an escape from my betting. I was really down, and so it came as a bit of a relief when I was given the green light to start training. Even when I started I had to build things up slowly. The physio John Porteous and the doctor were great at getting my fitness up, although I was always going to be playing catch-up because I hadn't got a full pre-season under my belt. I spent a few weeks doing all my running with John before I was finally able to get in with the rest of the lads.

I had to wait until 16 October 1999 before I finally made my debut for Motherwell. It came off the bench in a 2–2 draw with Hibs at Fir Park. I came into the team when we were struggling because we had only won once in our first seven league games. It was funny because we were second-bottom of the league, but we were still well ahead of Ebbe Skovdahl's Aberdeen. The Dons were a big club but they were really toiling and hadn't won a single game. They came to Fir Park in our next fixture and it is a game that will be remembered for a long, long time.

I came off the bench in what turned out to be an epic encounter which we lost 6–5. There were eleven goals, including hat-tricks for Spenny and Aberdeen's Robbie Winters, in a match that saw Andy Goram in goals at one end and Jim Leighton at the other

– two of the greatest goalkeepers that Scotland has ever seen. That match was just so surreal, watching the goals fly in from the bench, and playing in it was just as mind-blowing. Aberdeen went 6–3 ahead and we rallied at the death. Aberdeen were rocking, and I think if we had been given another couple of minutes we would have at least taken a draw. I still can remember looking at the scoreboard and shaking my head as we trooped off the pitch.

The good thing, from my point of view, is that I got my first start in the league when we made the trip to Tannadice on the Saturday. We managed to register only our second win thanks to goals from John Spencer and Shaun Teale, who netted a penalty. That gave us a fair bit of confidence for another away trip, as we made the short trip to the east end of Glasgow to take on Celtic. We went there and nobody really gave us a chance. It is quite funny because as a player you always know that the odds are stacked against you when you go to places like Celtic Park and Ibrox.

I scored early on after fifteen minutes. I can still remember the goal like it was five minutes ago. 'The Goalie' rolled the ball out to Stevie McMillan. He took about five paces forward. I dragged Stiliyan Petrov wide, and Stevie threaded a ball between two defenders. I spun and ran through and screamed a shot high past Jonathan Gould. It was an amazing feeling.

I have friends, Stevie and Danny Curran, who I gave complimentary tickets to that night. They were big Celtic fans but they had got stuck in traffic and had been late in getting into the ground. They walked into the stadium just as my goal went in. They were big Celtic fans but I knew they were also at the game to support me. Stevie is still one of my best mates and has been to a lot of my games. I know it was big for him because he still talks about my goal and that night.

We were 1–0 up and I thought we had a wee chance of maybe getting something. Celtic, as expected, turned the screw and left us camped in our own half as they pushed for an equaliser. It was like the Alamo at times. We weren't helped by the fact that Shaun Teale got sent off after thirty-four minutes for a foul on Mark Burchill. That saw John Barnes's side come out and pound us. I was meant to be playing as a winger, but I spent the rest of the game after I had scored playing left-back beside McMillan. I remember we went in 1–0 at half time, and I think even the manager was in a state of disbelief by the fact we were winning. I remember Billy Davies told us just to go out and give it a go in the second half, knowing fine we would be up against it. He signed off by saying, 'Don't worry about things because these aren't the games that matter. If you take anything from this game then it is a bonus.' Fair play to the manager, because he took the pressure right off us by using a bit of reverse psychology.

'The Goalie' was absolutely unbelievable for us that night. That was the best game I have ever seen him play. It is funny, he played out of his skin and I ended up getting the Man of the Match award because of my goal. Andy should definitely have got it. I was just amazed at what a good goalkeeper he was. I knew he had been a top keeper for Rangers, Hibs and Scotland, but it wasn't until I played and trained with him that I actually realised how good he was. Some of the saves he made that night were world class.

I got taken off in the later stages, and it was a nervous ten minutes sitting on the bench. I was back to biting my nails again. I was also completely done in, I was that bad that I wasn't even able to train on the Thursday. We won the game, and it was an amazing feeling at the final whistle. For once, I had burst a few coupons rather than it being the other way about. The dressing room at the end of the game was a mix of joy and disbelief, the fact we had won despite having played the majority of the game with ten men. I had to go up and do the press conference, and I had never seen so many journalists and radio broadcasters in all my life. It was a great feeling and that was the first time I felt I had shown my worth and I could play alongside all these top players at Motherwell. It is also the game for Motherwell most of the fans will remember me for.

It was obviously a real highlight for me. It was also good for my friends and family, although they all give me stick when I mention that goal from time to time. 'The Goalie' also wrote about it in his latest book and said that it was one of the biggest wins of his career. I am still big friends with Andy, and we keep in regular touch. He jokes that I still text him at eight o'clock on 27 October every year to remind him of my goal. It was also mentioned in my best man's speech, thanks to Craig Dargo and Elliott Smith, so there is no getting away from it. It is something that not many people have done, scoring the only goal at Parkhead. My career has been blighted by gambling, but that goal is something that can never be taken away from me.

You might not believe this, but I didn't even have money on myself to score or for Motherwell to win against Celtic that night. My dad, though, did have a punt on me. He stuck £5 on me to score at 33–1, so at least he got a decent return on me. I think that must have been the solitary time in my football career where I actually won him money. Normally I was taking it off my parents, although it was mainly my mum.

Another wee poignant note from that game involved Alan MacDonald, our kit man. I grew really close to Alan when I was at Fir Park and I think that bond grew stronger because of my goal at Parkhead. I remember he told me how his dad was really ill but they managed to take him to the game. Sadly, that was the last match he made it to because he passed away not long after it. I remember feeling quite emotional when Alan told me that story. He joked that at least I helped his dad die a happy man.

The manager was also brilliant and he gave me a lot of confidence with the belief he showed in me. He told me that Celtic Park had been a good grounding for me, and it was now about getting fitter and stronger. My fitness was still pretty poor because I was still playing catch-up after my bout of glandular fever. I think he was happy that a player he had gambled on from the lower leagues had shown he could take the step up. My good form continued as I scored the only goal of the game that weekend as we beat my old team St Johnstone 1–0 at Fir Park. Those goals helped get my career at Motherwell off to a flyer. Suddenly, that run of games turned our season on its head. We had gone from the bottom end and were suddenly up to fourth and fighting it out for one of the European places.

It was a really good spell for the club and me personally. I built up a good rapport with the fans and with everybody at the club. There was also such a good team behind the scenes at Fir Park. I was well looked after. There was one afternoon in a match against St Johnstone where I almost reduced my fan club by a couple of followers. It was just one of these mad moments. I took a shot while I was warming up out on the pitch at half time. I missed the goal and it flew into the stand and hit a pregnant woman. I didn't see it hit the lady, but I saw the commotion it caused. There were stewards and fans round her. I went over to see if she was okay and her husband started to go mental at me. It was an accident, and I felt really bad but I could understand why he started going mad at me. I would probably have done the same thing if I had been in his position, but it was a genuine accident.

I was distraught. I will never forget it. I got the couple to leave their name and contact details at the club so I could get in touch with them after the game. I was pretty upset when I went back inside. The manager found out what had happened and the physio, John Porteous, could see how it had affected me. They pulled me aside and told me I had to put it out of my mind and concentrate on my football. That was easier said than done because I was more concerned that the lady and her baby were okay. Betty Pryde, the manager's secretary, organised for the couple to come in and meet me at the ground the following week. I got the team to sign a top for them and I was just relieved when I was told the mum and baby-to-be were both okay. They were both massive Motherwell fans. I was just delighted to get the chance to say sorry and to make sure they were all okay.

We won that game 2–1 and we were battling it out with Hearts for third place and the final UEFA Cup place. We had been as high as third, but Hearts were also a good experienced team and they managed to keep their noses in front of us. We lost to Dundee United and Aberdeen, but a superb free-kick from Ged Brannan gave us a point at home against Celtic. I then netted a double in our 2–0 win over Hibs. With my background it was always good to score against the Hibees. We beat Dundee United, and it meant the race for Europe went down to the final game. We were due to play Rangers at Fir Park while Hearts had an Edinburgh derby to finish things off. That afternoon, believe me, I was a Hibs fans for probably the only time in my life. The odds were certainly stacked against us. We were up against the champions, although the league had already been well wrapped up before that final day.

I wasn't happy with the manager before the game because he pulled me in and told me I was on the bench. I was devastated because it was such a massive game for the club. I felt I had done well against Dundee United, I had set up one of Don Goodman's goals, but it wasn't enough to keep me in the team.

The manager, to his credit, said that he was going to set up his team to defend like mad, and he believed I could come on and make an impact in the final thirty minutes, when we could open up and go for a winner. At the time I felt he had fobbed me off and that was just an excuse. He told me that he might be wrong but believed that was the best way to approach the game. It was so funny because that was exactly how the game panned out. It was as if the manager had a crystal ball.

I came on with about thirty minutes to go and with just about my first touch I scored to put us 1–0 up. Things got even better when I helped to set up our second for John Spencer. We were delighted come the final whistle, but that joy soon turned to despair when Hearts beat Hibs to clinch third spot and left us outwith the European places. It was a real body blow. My boyhood team, Hearts, had made Europe, but that was no consolation to me. I wasn't interested. My focus had all been on Motherwell, and I had so wanted to help us get into Europe, especially for the manager, but we fell just short and it was a sore one to take.

10

SCOTLAND STARS PAST AND PRESENT: SPENNY AND THE GOALIE TO JIG AND FADDY

John 'Spenny' Spencer was a real character. Spenny was at the centre of most of the dressing-room pranks and stitch-ups when he was there. The one afternoon that stands out for me was during a club open day for the fans. There were loads of police and stewards about the ground to keep all the fans in order. They got to watch us train and then after that we had to go round and meet the supporters, sign autographs and pose for pictures.

After we had finished training, Alan MacDonald, the kit man, got the club mini-bus so he could drive us round to the gym at the other side of the ground. We jumped on the bus and on the front seat there was a walkie-talkie. I don't know how it got there or who it belonged to. The next thing we knew, Spenny had picked it up and was talking into it, mimicking the voice of a long-distance truck driver hitting the highway. We were all in hysterics as he gave it. 'Stewards to the boot room, stewards to the boot room, we have an incident.'

We thought it was a laugh and a joke, but little did we know that he had sparked a major incident. A lot of the police and stewards had raced to the boot room and the home dressing room to see what was happening. When they got there, of course, they were left totally bemused, as there was nothing and no one there.

We then got round to the gym and started to sign autographs for the fans. The next thing we knew, two police officers came up and lifted Spenny. They left him sitting in the back of this police car for half an hour, and I think he thought he was heading for the local police station. He ended up getting a right ticking off because he had sparked a major security alert. Spenny was just mad.

You had to watch your back when John was going about because he was a constant menace, although he is also one of the funniest guys I have come across in my life. He is just so full of life and so down to earth for a player who had starred at the very highest level. The only thing where he really was flash was when it came to his watches. They were so expensive that he used to go through and ask Betty Pryde, the manager's secretary, to put them into the club safe before he went out training. I am laughing, but one of his watches could well have cleared my gambling debts for a few years.

Andy 'The Goalie' Goram was another big personality. There were times when you wouldn't even see him at training for two or three days. He would then come in on the Friday and would be absolutely brilliant – he looked like he had been training all week. The standards he set himself were just incredible. I don't know how he was able to go on some of the drinking sessions he did and still be able to produce the goods. He trained the way he played; he demanded perfection and 100 percent from everybody round him.

I ended up on quite a few of his tongue-lashings during some of our training sessions. There were a couple of times where I had been a bit slack and lazy, I hadn't tracked my man back and then he had crossed and the other team had scored. The Goalie would go mad. He would come out and start screaming and shouting at me. I have never seen anyone like him, but that was just his professionalism. My attitude was at the opposite end of the scale. I would just shrug my shoulders and think to myself, 'What is he getting so excited about? It is only training.' That was where we differed, and that was why he played at the highest level and I never did.

I have seen a lot of good goalkeepers in my career, from Antti Niemi, Craig Gordon, Scott Thomson and Alan Main, but The Goalie was head and shoulders above them all. Nobody was a patch on him. He was something else. I think he could have been one of the best goalkeepers ever had he not taken his eye off the ball at times with his heavy drinking sessions. He was also linked with a Scotland recall when he was at Motherwell. His form was certainly good enough, but I think a combination of politics and a collection of his off-the-field headlines meant that was never going to materialise. I know he got his move to Manchester United, but that was at the tail end of his career. He played for United and I was delighted for him when he made that move, but I just think he should have been playing for a team like United or another big English club when he was in his prime. Andy has since come out and admitted he has a drinking problem. I know his character, and I am in no doubt that is one battle he can fight and win.

My manager Billy Davies was also absolutely fantastic to me. He was so full of fun, and as a coach he was tactically astute. Many of the techniques most of the top clubs are introducing now are things he had already brought into Motherwell. He introduced dieticians and regular fitness tests. He was also massive on doing core work, but I never really had that until I arrived at Fir Park. Billy was so intelligent. He wanted to learn and he amassed so much information going and learning from other coaches and managers all across the world. He fed off everyone, but he was always down to earth and had so much time for everyone.

If you were playing well then he would tell you, and in the same way he would let you know if he didn't think you were producing the goods. He could be volatile if the team weren't producing it on the park, but that was only because he wanted the best for everyone at the club. He went absolutely mental at us after that game we lost 6–5 to Aberdeen. He went mad at the way we had defended. He let us know it was completely unacceptable. I was fine with that because I knew any criticism that came my way was to try and make me become a better player. He was very honest and straight to the point. There was no rubbish or flannel with him. He laid it on the line and told you how it was. As a person and manager, I thought he was fantastic. I could have gone and talked to quite a few of my managers, but Billy was probably the one I felt closest to. I also believe that if I had gone to him and said I had a problem with gambling then he would have helped me out, because that was the type of person he was.

Personally, he was a bit like a father figure to me. Billy, Spenny and Goram looked after me when I first went to Motherwell. Billy, in particular, was first class. He looked after me and he also made sure my family and people round me were fine. When my mum or dad used to come through for games he would always take time out to speak to them and make sure they were okay. That meant a lot to me.

I was always confident that Billy was going to move on to bigger and better things. It has been good watching him progress his managerial career. I have followed him closely since he left Motherwell. He did well on a limited budget at Preston North End and then he moved on to Derby County and got them into the Premier League. He then went on to Nottingham Forest and took them from the relegation zone of the Championship and turned them into play-off regulars. He has done well at every club he has been at and that is no coincidence because he is a top manager.

Billy was often accused of nepotism during his time at Motherwell, but nothing could have been further from the truth. The finger was pointed at him because John Spencer was his brother-in-law and he also signed his brother John Davies. Both were exceptional players, but it would have been unfair to say any of them got preferential treatment. In fact, there were times when Billy would go the other way, especially when it came to his brother John. It was funny because Billy used to give him pelters during some of our training sessions and more often than not it would end up in a family feud. It was funny because we would be back in the dressing room and John would still be fuming and would say things like, 'See if he wasn't family.' It gave the rest of the lads a right few laughs.

I became really friendly with John Davies. He also liked a gamble and was involved in quite a lot of my betting at Motherwell. I used to go to the racing with him, and I could also put a lot of bets on with him as well. He would phone them in via the betting contacts and accounts he had. That would allow me to really pile up the debt. It went as high as £7,000 to £8,000 at one stage and he had to wait for a long time to get the money he was due. It normally got to a stage where I would get my monthly wages and I would have to hand it over to John so I could try to clear my debts. John loved the racing scene. He was well connected and he also got a lot of tips from time to time, which always came in handy. I have seen John a few times since I left Motherwell, and he is another fantastic guy who would do anything for you.

Billy Davies also got on amazingly well with David 'Ned' Kelly. That is how it isn't really a surprise that they have gone on to work together in management. Ned had played at the highest level and was very well respected by the rest of the players at the club. He was a really nice guy and his playing curriculum vitae spoke for itself. He had played and produced the goods at the highest level in England and internationally with the Republic of Ireland.

Another player at the opposite end of the age spectrum was Lee McCulloch. Hearts bid £1 million for Lee McCulloch when I was at Motherwell with him. The club felt he was worth more and that was why he didn't go. He was still a young kid at the time and I spoke to him a bit about Hearts. I told him how they were a big club and it would be a decent move for him, but I think Billy Davies had already spoken to him and told him to hang fire because there were bigger things on the horizon. There were a few clubs who were interested in 'Jig' during my time at Fir Park, and it was hardly a surprise.

Lee is a great lad. He was football daft. He was a young boy but he was quite mature for his age. He was also really family-orientated and a very nice guy. Lee was your perfect centre-forward. He was good in the air, offered a physical presence and he also had a decent touch for such a big lad. He was the main striker, but he always had good experienced players round him, like John Spencer and Don Goodman. Spenny used to spend a lot of time with him out on the training field. He would always try to get him to get into the box a bit more, to score more goals and get in around the six-yard box. To be fair to Jig, he was a decent finisher when the ball dropped to him inside the box. Most of his goals were screamers from distance. He never scored a lot of your typical poacher's goals. That was why he got the nickname 'Jig', because the joke was that he used to fall apart when he got into the box. He did a lot of unselfish work for the team. He was really hardworking and that is why he had a lot of people who were really interested in him.

I also used to socialise quite a bit with Lee and Ged Brannan. A lot of the time we were going out, I had to borrow money from them just to get a few drinks in. I borrowed a bit of money off quite a few of the boys. Ged never really struggled for money. He had played at Manchester City. He had earned quite a bit of money and had also invested wisely. Ged was also a very kind-hearted person and he would always help me out wherever he could. He was a good friend to have, but like most of my team-mates, he didn't know the full extent of my gambling. The funny thing is that he had a lot of money but he hardly gambled. That was probably why he was well-off. He would occasionally put a bet on if he got a tip for a horse, but he certainly wasn't a big gambler. I don't think I ever saw Lee in the bookies either.

I have kept in touch with them both since we moved on with our lives and careers, and the stories from our time together are hard to forget. For instance, there was one stage where I asked to borrow £1,000 off Ged. It was at a time when I was in a right state. Thankfully I never ended up taking the money because it was just before I came to the end of the road with my gambling. I know Ged would have given me the money without even asking what it was for, because he was that sort of guy. To be fair, though, Ged was one of the few guys I actually did pay back.

I remember the day a helicopter landed on the halfway line at Fir Park to take Lee McCulloch and Stevie McMillan down to Wigan Athletic. It was near the end of the 2000–01 season, my second season at Fir Park. Lee and Stevie's careers were ready to hit the heights, while as for Motherwell and me, we were heading off in a different direction.

That was the beginning of the end as the big names started to exit. The club were in a real transitional phase. We could all sense that things weren't right behind the scenes. Billy Davies wanted to take the team on. He had set his sights higher and higher and maybe deep down, although he never said as much, he probably thought he could have had Motherwell splitting the Old Firm. If you look at the team we had that first season I was there, then he certainly had the basis to do it. Maybe if he had been allowed to bring in one or two more quality players then you never know what could have happened. Unfortunately, nobody will ever know because the club were forced to cut their wage bill. They were spending money they didn't have and that was to come back and haunt them later. We were paying big wages and that point was the start of a massive downward spiral. We maybe should have realised then that the club were in a mess. They were paying players £8,000 to £10,000 a week, and that was well outwith their means.

The good thing from the club and the fans' point of view, was that they turned to their youth ranks and gave them a chance. That was the obvious way the club were going to be able to reduce their wage bill and at the same time generate future funds. I suppose that was where Motherwell were quite fortunate. They had the raw talent coming through and all the boys needed was a bit of first-team exposure to show everyone they were good enough.

It is no coincidence that most of the young boys that Billy Davies took in at Motherwell went on to have decent careers. Guys like Stevie Hammell, James McFadden, Keith Lasley, Stephen Pearson and Shaun Fagan were all nurtured in the right way. Billy knew when the time was right to bring them in. Motherwell had a great intake of young players around that time. That was all credit to Dave McParland, who headed up the youth ranks. He was also assisted by Paul Smith. These guys were responsible for bringing the likes of McFadden, Paul Quinn, David Clarkson, Pearson and Hammell to the club. Others try to take credit for spotting them, but if you ask any of these boys then they will say it would have been down to Paul and McParland. I also know that McFadden was actually put out of the door at one stage, and if it hadn't been for Paul, then he might never have turned into the Motherwell and Scotland legend he has become. Paul and Dave both had such an eye for a player. I am actually surprised that Paul hasn't been offered a full-time job at another Scottish Premier League club. His record speaks for itself, and since he has left Motherwell, he has been scouting for Gretna and Queen of the South. I have also had a few nights out with him and got to know his family really well. I also – surprise, surprise – had a good few nights out at the casino with him and Roberto Martinez.

When James McFadden first broke onto the scene, John Spencer was desperate to cut off his ponytail. He had grown the ponytail since he was a wee boy but Spenny just thought it looked daft and needed to be cut off. A lot of the boys wanted to get a hold of him and cut it off, but I remember the manager warned the rest of the boys not to do it because it meant so much to him. Thankfully, none of the boys did, because I think it would probably have ended up causing a riot in the dressing room.

'Faddy' was a typical Glasgow boy. He was a wee boy who was full of confidence and he had such unquestionable ability even as a youngster. James got to train with the first team when he was still a young kid, showing what a talent he had. He is the most talented young kid I have seen, without a shadow of a doubt. James might have got to train with the rest of the boys, but he also had his duties to do as well. He didn't shirk them either. He was a really good worker, did his stuff and was willing to learn. He would never moan about cleaning the boots and mopping the dressing room. That is probably one of the reasons he has gone so far in the game. He has had a great career with Scotland and in England with Everton and Birmingham. James has been a wee bit unlucky with injuries, and I think they have curtailed him from going even higher. He was also a lovely kid and deserves all the success that comes his way.

Stevie Hammell was a great wee lad. He was another player who would go on and make a decent name for himself. Hammell did really well at Motherwell before he moved down to Southend. I thought he might have gone higher in England but he decided for whatever reason to return to Motherwell. He has been a real stalwart for the club, and it is no surprise to see him being rewarded with a testimonial. He has been a real loyal servant to Motherwell. I remember when I first came across him he made a real impression. He was like a wee bear when you faced up to him in training. He was just so strong and he was another who had a fantastic attitude. He loved his football and was always willing to listen and learn.

Stephen Pearson also came in around that time. What I recall was that he was like a skeleton. He hardly had an ounce of fat on him. He was almost abnormal when we did the body fat testing. Stephen was also so fit. He was like a machine; he could run all day. He was your modern-day midfielder. He was box-to-box and was also a decent finisher. He started to be linked with teams before Motherwell even went into administration. Stephen was also a really nice guy, but to be fair, so were all the boys at the club, including Keith Lasley, Dougie Ramsay and Shaun Fagan. They were a good set of boys, and that is why they have all gone on to have decent careers for them-selves.

We finished eighth that second season, and I think everybody could see we were going to slide back. It was an impossible job to try and emulate that first season's success. You only had to look at how much the wage bill had been cut. It really was night and day, and all the new arrivals were on a fraction of what their big-earning predecessors had picked up. I really felt for the fans because I thought we were on the verge of something big, but the chairman, John Boyle, had decided he had ploughed enough into the club and had to try and run them on a more self-sustainable model.

The other person I really felt for was the manager Billy Davies. He is a hugely ambitious person. He wants the best, and I sensed that from the first moment I met him. Then when I started to work under him, he continually wanted to raise the bar and improve everything at the club. I honestly think he believed that with a bit more backing he could have got Motherwell up challenging or even splitting the Old Firm. Let's not forget that he helped Motherwell do it as a player, when they finished second to Rangers in the 1993–94 season under Alex McLeish. Sadly under him, though, it wasn't to be. The club had lived outwith their means and had started to struggle financially, even failing to pay some of their major bills. I had started to get a flavour of things in some of my conversations with Pat Nevin, though he never told me how bad the situation was, even though at the end he did warn me to get out if I could.

At the start of the 2001–02 season, it was all change at Fir Park. We had the youngsters but we also lacked a bit of experience, and Billy had to go out and raid the bargain basements to get players. No disrespect to the players who came in, but they weren't at the same level as their predecessors, despite the fact they were all decent players in their own right with half-decent pedigrees. Young Mark Brown, who had played for

Rangers, came in to replace Andy Goram, while the former QPR defender Karl Ready and ex-Bolton centre-half Greg Strong were recruited, and Roberto Martinez arrived from Wigan Athletic, Eddie Forrest from Airdrie and Andy Dow came down from Aberdeen. I ended up being one of the bigger names left at the club. The club was very much in a transitional period. A lot of the fans were left a little bit bewildered because they had let all the big stars go and they replaced them with players who were good, but maybe didn't have the same profiles as the ones they were asked to replace. It was a part of a dark period for the club and for many of the boys.

I could see what was happening to the club, the standard of the squad and where we were going, but that didn't bother me. I was more concerned about picking up my money so I could gamble or throw it all away.

If I had any sense about me, I should have moved on rather than signing my new contract. I could probably have gone to England, but I was in a comfort zone earning good money and I didn't see any point in moving. However, I didn't think the club would fall as far as it did.

11

MADNESS IN MOTHERWELL

I was still living in Edinburgh well into my second season at Motherwell. I was staying in a flat in Dalkeith with Jill and our daughter Emma. It was hardly ideal, especially as I couldn't drive, but I was more than happy remaining close to my friends and family. Also I was quite fortunate because most of the time I would get a lift through from the Motherwell chief executive Pat Nevin. He lived in Duns, and he would pick me up on his way up to Fir Park. On the days he didn't go in I would have to get up early and head through on the train. It was a bit of a trek, but to be fair, Pat took me through most of the time and went out of his way to ferry me up and down the M8.

Pat and I spent a lot of time together travelling, and we became really close. He was another hero of mine. Pat was a winger like myself (although there was a bit of a height difference), but he had still played for some big clubs like Chelsea and Everton, and also for Scotland. He was a player I had always admired and appreciated. He always had time for me and we became good friends. It was a good education listening to Pat. He tried to teach me good habits and would give me pointers on how I could improve my game.

The travelling, however, eventually started to grind me down, and I thought if I was going to give my football 100 percent then I needed to move to Motherwell. I felt I owed it to the club and myself to move through so I could give my all. I had about six months left on my contract when the club offered me a new deal. A lot of the big names had left the club: Steve McMillan, Ged Brannan and Lee McCulloch were all sold to Wigan, while Andy Goram had left for Manchester United and John Spencer also announced he was leaving for America's Major League Soccer because the club had to cut their spiralling wage bill.

Pat Nevin was dealing with a lot of the financial sides of things at the club. He had given me a fair idea of the direction the club was going (that is, dramatically reducing their spending) in some of our many journeys from the capital to Lanarkshire. Pat told me things could work in my favour. He said it would be a chance to sign on again and become one of the main players at the club. I was offered a fair increase to stay, and I didn't need to be asked twice. One or two other teams had been sniffing around, but I was more than happy to remain at Motherwell, especially as I was being offered vastly improved terms. I went up to something like £2,000 a week basic. I was also due to get £60,000 in signing-on fees and then there were good bonuses and appearance money on top of that. Finances, if I hadn't been gambling, should have been the least of my concerns at that stage. The club also pushed their initial offer up from two to three years. It was too good a deal to turn down. I was earning a lot more than at any time in my career, and I was also set to become one of the highest earners at the club.

I spoke to Jill and she agreed we had to give it a go and move through to Motherwell. We also had to get a school sorted for Emma, which had to be our main priority. I managed to get her into Dalziel High School. It is one of the top schools in the area and it was near impossible to get your child in there. I, however, managed to pull a few strings, but only because the headmaster was a massive Motherwell fan. I went in and spoke to him and we had a brief twenty-minute meeting. I don't even think the school or Emma was mentioned because he just wanted to know what was going on at Fir Park.

The next step was to buy a new house or flat. We had a look about and there was a new-build estate just down the road from Fir Park that caught our eye. It was perfect for Emma's school, and it was also handy for me to get up to the ground. I knew deep down, however, that finding a new home was the easy part, but paying for it was another story all together. I knew myself I would have next to no chance of getting a mortgage because of my credit rating, debts and my gambling addiction. To this day I still don't know how we got that mortgage. It had next to nothing to do with me; it was all down to Jill. She had loads of savings, worked a couple of jobs and she had got the money together. If it was down to me then I would have struggled to have enough left in my pocket at the end of the week to pay for a cardboard box. I had a lot of debts and my name was also blacklisted because I hadn't been paying loans back. We managed to get everything signed and sealed, and it was good because we had got a half-decent deal on the house, and we knew that if we had to sell it in the short term then we would be guaranteed to at least make a decent profit. If I am being honest, it was money I was keen to get my hands on right away.

Signing that new contract at Motherwell ended up being the beginning of the end for me. I had this extra money and I started to gamble like never before. It wasn't just my wages I was gambling, but I was also taking even more loans out. They weren't just personal loans but loans against our new family home. I was borrowing money against the house, even though it was a joint mortgage and Jill didn't know a thing about any of it. I could have left her and Emma out on the street, and I didn't even have the decency to tell them or even warn them. It was crazy and inexcusable, but I was out of control. My financial situation was so bad that the everyday high street banks wouldn't even look at me or even consider giving me a loan or any more money. I had to start looking down some murky and more costly avenues.

I started to take out loans from finance companies, the type you see on television every day, even though I was having to pay astronomical amounts back in interest. I wasn't even considering the consequences or what I would have to pay back. I just wanted my hands on hard cash that I could hand over the counter to a bookie or throw down in chips on a roulette table.

There was one day I went in person to a finance company in Hamilton. Some of their staff were a bit surprised to see a footballer in a place like that. I remember walking in, and I didn't care who knew me, I just wanted the money. I could sense people questioning why I was there. I was earning big money as a footballer – it was a lot more than your average wage – and I should have had more than enough to live on comfortably. I shouldn't have needed to take a loan from somewhere like that. I was just so desperate to get money that I would have done near enough anything.

I think I got a loan of £10,000 cash that day. I had only taken out a short-term loan but their interest rates were astronomical. You can see why people can get into real trouble by taking loans from these sort of companies, although I know these sort of lenders will argue that their rates are in all their adverts for everyone to see in black and white. I think I had to end up paying £15,000 back in interest, so I had to end up giving them £25,000 in total. It was utter madness. I wasn't even thinking about the long-term consequences for Jill, Emma or myself. I was only interested in the here and now and how I could get money to bet and blow. I also got to the point where I wasn't even looking at the bigger picture. I was getting money but I was no longer paying off my outstanding debts or loans. Every bean I had was being gambled, pure and simple.

Football was very much secondary to my betting. I still went out and gave my all during the games, but I couldn't say I was 100 percent committed when it came to training. Andy Dow, who arrived from Aberdeen, was my partner in crime during my final season at Motherwell. I don't even know if he knew how bad my gambling problem was. I am sure he must have had some idea. I went to training every day as a footballer, but if I am being honest with you, I just couldn't wait to get away to bet. When I was at Motherwell I used to go to Coral's every day. I had started going to the Ladbrokes in the city centre, but I used to get too much hassle in there. I bet a lot in there in my first season but it was too central and too many people knew who I was. Fans and fellow punters would come up and ask me about what was happening at Motherwell, but I wasn't interested in small talk, I just wanted to bet and I didn't want to be distracted from that next race or match.

Andy Dow and I started to go to another bookies in a housing estate in the middle of nowhere, where nobody could see me. As soon as training was finished, we went straight to the bookies. We would also be regulars at the Hamilton races. I knew Bert Logan, who used to be at Hearts, who was a regular bookie at the racecourses. He would give us better odds because he knew us and we were putting such vast sums of money on. I was walking about thinking I was better than anybody else because I was getting 4–1 instead of 3–1. I thought I had hit gold but the only person sitting laughing was Bert because nine times out of ten my horse would be nowhere near the winner's post, and I was handing over anything from £500 to £5,000. Bert will be sitting today counting his money while I left myself with nothing.

It wasn't just £100 or £200 bets, I was handing over bundles of notes that would have choked a horse or even paid my mortgage for three or four months. Even when my horse did come in, then it just went back to Bert because I would punt that to try and win even more. The money didn't matter to me because it was all about the buzz of the bet rather than the money or winning.

Andy and I became really close, as did Jill and Andy's wife Sarah. We went to the bookies most days, but I knew Andy could have quite easily stopped betting. He was doing it more for something to do and to keep me company; I was doing it because it was the be-all and end-all. There were times when Andy didn't go to the bookies and I would end up going by myself and getting one of my teammates to drop me off on their way home.

It is so ironic because one of the cashiers in that Coral's bookies was the same man who had served me over the previous two years. He had seen how much money I had lost, thousands and thousands of pounds. It came to a head one afternoon when he told me he couldn't really take much more money off me. He said he was starting to feel really sorry for me because I was going down such a bad road. He then told me his own son played professional football and he said that he also thought he had a bit of a problem with gambling. He said he felt for me and didn't want to see my gambling getting even worse. I would estimate he had taken tens of thousands off me in bets over the previous year or so. I had handed over the majority of my wages and all my signing-on fees and a lot extra on top of that.

The man was only looking out for me, but his words were like a red rag to a bull. I said to him, 'Who do you think you are, telling me what to do?' Even after the man had tried to offer a helping hand, I had thrown the offer back in his face. I continued going to the same bookies but I would try to go to other cashiers rather than face him. I still speak to his son regularly and I have a good relationship with him. Thinking back to how I treated his dad still makes me feel bad, but it has also made me realise how lucky I am still to have my dad. It has helped make my relationship with my own dad even more special.

Back then, I gave very little thought to my own family, never mind anybody else's. I continued to blow absolute fortunes, and I wasn't really concerned if there was food in the fridge or enough in the bank to pay the mortgage. Jill would have to go through to Edinburgh and even work nights. She was working all hours of the day to make ends meet. I was making thousands and she hardly saw a penny. I was hardly a model parent either. Emma would come home from school and I'd leave her sitting outside because I was in the bookies. It wouldn't just be for ten or fifteen minutes, I was talking hours. She would phone me constantly, asking me, 'Where are you?' I kept telling her I would be home shortly, but I never was.

I will tell you how messed up I was. I could go into the bookies one day with £1,000 and I might be there for six or seven hours and still have £50 in my pocket. On rare days I did, I felt like a lottery winner because I still had money, even though I had lost £950. I would swan home and walk into the house like the king of the manor. I might give Emma £10 and I say, 'Don't worry about dinner. I will get it tonight. I'll phone a takeaway.' That was how deluded I was. Looking back, it was ridiculous. I was an embarrassment.

12

BLACK DAYS AT THE 'WELL

It didn't help that, as I continued to throw good money after bad, Motherwell also decided to gamble on change. Billy Davies, the man who had signed me and given me my chance in the top flight, left and Eric Black came in and took over, along with Terry Butcher as his assistant and Chris McCart heading up the youth set-up. I was devastated when Billy got the sack. I was really gutted. I was not only losing a manager but a guy who had been like a father figure in my early days at the club. I didn't see it coming. I didn't think the club would have sacked him. The only way I saw that happening was because Billy was a strong character. He would never have backed down to anyone. I don't think he was happy with the level of backing he was getting to bring in other players. The club hadn't matched his ambitions.

Billy has gone on to show what a top manager he is. He has done so well down south. As mentioned earlier, he took Preston North End into the Championship play-offs, Derby County into the Premier League and Nottingham Forest into the play-offs as well. He still has plenty to offer and will end up with another big job, sooner rather than later. He wants the best and he isn't afraid to speak up for himself. We all saw that at Nottingham Forest when he walked out after they refused to match his ambitions. He wants the best. When he takes a job he puts his heart and soul into it and he looks for the same in return. He obviously challenged John Boyle and ended up getting the sack. I think he knew that when he left Motherwell that he wouldn't be short of options.

The man who had signed me had left, and suddenly a new man was set to come in. That sort of transition does leave a bit of uncertainty. You don't know if the next manager is going to fancy you, but that is part and parcel of football. I still had confidence in my ability outwith my off-the-field issues. I was the captain of the team and a main player when Billy Davies left, but that all changed when the club brought in the former Aberdeen striker and ex-Celtic coach Eric Black as our new manager. He brought in the former Rangers captain Terry Butcher as his assistant. Within weeks, I knew I wasn't in their plans.

The club were looking to downsize, and I knew that because Pat Nevin had already told me as much. The chairman, John Boyle, had invested a lot of money in the club and the collapse of the Setanta television deal meant he had to pull the horns in a bit. I was one of the higher earners and I knew Black was going to come in with his own ideas. He had been working as an agent before he took the job, and it quickly became apparent that he wanted to go down the route of bringing in a lot of foreign players. Black basically came in and told most of the higher earners, including myself, that we were no longer wanted at the club. He told me personally it would be better for all concerned if I found a new club. I was really unhappy with the way he handled my situation. I had not long signed a new contract and I was only twelve months into it. I still had nearly two years left to go, and I was never going to just get up and walk away from a basic of more than £100,000 a year just because the manager wanted me out. It ended up in a bit of a stalemate.

I refused to budge, and Black got more and more frustrated with me. I think he was desperate to get me off the books so he could bring his own players in. I think he thought I was being deliberately awkward, but I wasn't. I genuinely didn't want to leave Motherwell. I was happy and I wanted to fight for my place, but Black made it clear that was never going to happen. It seemed that I wasn't in his plans and it didn't matter what I did on the training ground or pitch because that situation was never going to change. I don't think he liked the fact that I was pretty popular at the club. I got on well with all the staff, the players and the fans, and that seemed to annoy him.

Black continued to make it clear he wanted to bring in his own players. It didn't matter how well I was doing, I was a big earner, and I am in no doubt he wanted my wage to bring in three or four of his own players. As I mentioned, Black had been working as an agent before he took the Motherwell job, and I think he ended up bringing some of his own players in. I just found it strange. He brought in a lot of foreign players on less money, and they just weren't good enough. He had to do something to try to get the club moving forward but, as far as I'm concerned, his plan just didn't work. Maybe he had very few options, maybe he had been told to cut the budgets. I know some of the boys he was signing were on next to no money. I am talking about £300 to £400 a week. It was night and day to when I first arrived. When you are suddenly paying a fraction of the wages you were, then it is going to have a devastating impact on the team, and it did. The dressing room just totally changed. All the big stars and personalities had gone and now we had a lot of unknown foreign players. I know it must have been hard for them as well coming into a new environment, especially as some of them struggled to speak English. It was mainly guys who nobody had heard of and had been playing in some of the lower leagues in Europe. It is fair to say that only a handful of Black's signings were a success at Motherwell. The French defender Eric Deloumeaux came in and did well, as did the German and former Hibs striker Dirk Lehmann. They were the exceptions.

Ayr United came in for me and Eric Black asked me if I would go there to get some games, which would also put me in the shop window. Ayr were in the First Division and had a decent team. They were doing well and had also made the Co-operative Insurance Cup Final, where they were due to play Rangers. Gordon Dalziel was in charge, and he had been given a fair bit of money to spend and he was able to attract big names like John Hughes, James Grady and Pat McGinlay to Somerset Park. Ayr had a decent side, and it was probably a bit of contradiction at that stage of my life, joining a team nicknamed 'the Honest Men'.

I feel it suited Eric Black just to get me away from Fir Park and the boys, it also allowed him to free up some wages with the contribution Ayr were making to my contract. I went there on a short-term loan and probably the thrill and possibility of playing in the Cup final was the biggest carrot for me. I went there and trained for a couple of weeks and I also played in a game. We were in the build-up to the Cup final and I decided I couldn't play in that match at Hampden. I knew a lot of the boys would have resented me for coming in and taking a Cup final jersey from somebody who had worked so hard to get the team to that stage, it was one of the greatest days in the club's history and for a lot of the boys it would have been the biggest of their careers. Normally, as you would have gathered, it wouldn't have bothered me in the slightest, but I just felt it wasn't right to do that to somebody. I still don't know where that compassion came from. I felt like an outsider when I arrived, and that was understandable because they were a close-knit group and it was that unity that had helped to take them to Hampden. I certainly wouldn't have been happy if I had helped a team into a Cup final and then saw a loan signing come in and take my place on the big day. I thought about it for a few days, and I even discussed things with John Hughes when he drove me through from Edinburgh. I decided I didn't want to be there and morally I didn't think it was right to deny somebody a chance of Cup final glory.

I ended up going back to Motherwell, and it was fair to say that absence had failed to make the heart grow fonder when it came to Eric Black and me. It become personal, and he pretty much singled Andy Dow and me out because we were two of his highest earners and the players he wanted rid of. We were also close friends and he obviously thought that if we were not going to leave of our own accord, then he would sicken us and try to force us out the door. It became so petty and there was absolutely no need for it. Things then turned nasty. He made Andy and I come in at different times from the rest of the boys for training. He just didn't want us to have anything to do with the other players but it didn't really matter because I was still in regular contact with a lot of the other guys. He had Andy and me training with the kids. The manager would make sure we were well away from the ground before the first team came in for their sessions. He would have us up training on the Astroturf together and by the time we came back to the ground the first team were away.

That was his way of trying to bring Andy and me down, but it didn't work. What he did was help make me a stronger person and more determined to dig my heels in. Training with the kids was having no impact, so he made the pair of us train on our own. We had to be in at the ground to train at eight in the morning. We were in and away before the boys came in at 9.30 to 9.45. He would make us lap the park like Olympic long-distance runners. It was getting really, really stupid. Black would come out into the middle of the park and would watch us lapping the pitch. I used to wind him up. I would shout things like, 'Morning, gaffer. How are you? I really love running. It is a great morning. It really is doing wonders for my fitness.' I knew it got under his skin, and I could see him getting more and more annoyed, but I had decided there was no way I was going to give him the satisfaction of knowing he had won.

I just did everything that was asked of me, and I just smiled and got on with it. I did that until it came to the very end where Black really did go over the top. He realised the early morning sessions weren't working so he decided to take us in for after-noon sessions, once again, well after the rest of the first team had disappeared home. The youth coach, Chris McCart, also got involved in some of those sessions. He would take us down to Strathclyde Park and leave us to run round it. There were times where he wouldn't even watch us so I would end up spending most of my time in the amusements on the slot machines and then I would get a taxi back up to Fir Park. I would get dropped round the corner and would jog back to the ground. Or on other occasions I would phone a friend to come and pick Andy and me up. That is how ridiculous it got.

Terry Butcher would also take us up to Dalziel Park and would have us run round the track there. He would sit up in the starter's seat and would tell us to do 10,000 metres or twenty-five laps. Every time we passed him and did a lap he would put a stone down. Andy would race away but the longer it went on I thought, 'Stuff it,' and I would just jog round at my own leisurely pace. I used to take forever. I knew that got to Terry because he didn't want to be there either, and he was also desperate to get home.

In the end he got so cheesed off with me that he got off his seat, told us to do what we wanted and then stormed off. That was down to the fact that if I was being forced to run for three and a half hours, then Terry was going to have to sit and watch me for three and a half hours. Andy might have buckled, but I was never going to back down, that was one particular battle of wits I was determined to win.

I wasn't happy with the situation and I decided to get the Scottish Professional Footballers' Association in. I got in touch with the secretary and former Motherwell player Fraser Wishart to intervene on our behalf. I had been a good servant to Motherwell. I had kept my nose clean at the club and now through no fault of my own I was being treated like rubbish. I was still speaking to Pat Nevin, and he told me the club were really struggling financially. He said to me if I had the chance to leave, then I should take it. I knew the club were toiling, but I didn't realise how badly. Fraser came in and tried to sort things out, but, just days later, the club went into administration and the SPFA and Fraser had an even bigger problem on their hands.

Black's attitude toward some of the players wasn't great, especially the experienced players he had inherited from Billy Davies. A bust-up with David Kelly at Dunfermline was the perfect example of that. Black started blaming Ned for what had happened on the pitch, and he just flipped. What was said to David was well out of order. He was raging and he threw his boots down and said something back. Terry Butcher came up to him and they started slugging it out with each other. The boys had to end up getting in between them to split things up. That was another example of the way they thought they could get off with talking to people, guys who had played at the very highest level. Their man-management, out of all the people I have played under in my career, wasn't a patch on any of my previous coaches and managers, including Jimmy Thomson at Raith Rovers.

To be fair, Black, Butcher and McCart have gone on to make good names for themselves away from Motherwell. I wish them all the best. We have all moved on and I don't hold grudges, but my time under them wasn't a pleasant experience. I certainly didn't see eye to eye with them and probably never will.

13

BIN BAGS, ADMINISTRATION
AND THE DOLE

Motherwell had spent lavishly under John Boyle, trying to chase the dream of toppling or splitting the Old Firm. The Fir Park chairman had ploughed a lot of his own money into the club and had really raised its profile, especially when we had top stars like Andy Goram, John Spencer, Ged Brannan and Shaun Teale in our ranks. I think everyone knew that Motherwell were paying wages that the club could ill afford. It was always going to be unsustainable over the longer term, but everyone at the club enjoyed the ride while it lasted. There was always going to come a point when reality was going to hit home and the club was going to have to live within its means.

I think we saw that after we failed to make Europe in my first season, Boyle tried to cut the wage bill and one by one you saw the big stars begin to exit Fir Park. They were replaced with players on a fraction of the wages, although all guys who had a proven pedigree in the game. Then when Billy Davies left and was replaced by Eric Black, we really saw the cost-cutting hit home. The club ended up at the opposite end of the spectrum from when I had first arrived, paying a few hundred pounds to players. I think everyone knew then that it was pretty much the bust after the boom. I know Pat Nevin, the chief executive, was getting frustrated with the direction the club was going, and it certainly wasn't what he had signed up for when he had left Kilmarnock to become our director of football.

Pat was massive at the club for me. He was a friend as well as one of my bosses. After I had that chat with Pat, I went home and I spoke to Jill. I told her I thought there was something going on at the club. I just didn't realise how quickly the whole thing would blow up. Within two or three days it was all over the newspapers that we had gone into administration. That didn't really come as a complete surprise to me, but what was about to unfold really did shock me. I didn't have a clue what was going to happen to the club, the staff or even myself personally. I also didn't know how heartbreaking and brutal the administration process was going to be.

Initially, I wasn't really that concerned, probably because I had no idea of how the whole administration process worked. It was a relatively new thing within the realms of Scottish football. Looking back, I was so naive. I had a contract and as far as I was concerned it was watertight, regardless of what happened to the club. I still had two and a half years left on my deal, and I thought that if I was to get sacked I would get every penny I was due. I was so wet behind the ears. I thought I would be handed a cheque for the £240,000 and I could walk off to my next club. I didn't have the first clue about administration, how much financial trouble the club was in or the carnage that was about to ensue.

Reality soon hit home when I read up a bit more on administration. I quickly found out that I was unlikely to get all my money and there was also an alarming possibility that I might get nothing at all, although that was the worst-case scenario. When I heard that I feared I could be left behind the eight ball, with my gambling and the mess my life was in behind the scenes.

I had massive debts and I had put the house up as a guarantee for my loans without Jill knowing – that is how crazy I had been. Suddenly I could end up out of a job and my fiancée and daughter could end up out on their ear without a roof over their heads because of my sheer stupidity. The situation was a nightmare, yet my biggest concern wasn't my home or my family, it was how was I going to bet if I didn't have any money.

All the players and staff held a meeting with the main administrator, Bryan Jackson of PKF. He spoke to us all and basically talked us through the administration process. He said he was going to sift through all the club's finances and warned us that some of the players might be okay, but for others it would be the end of the road at Motherwell. That proved to be exactly the case.

The administrators announced there would be redundancies and moved the cull forward twenty-four hours to try and keep the press off the scent. The axe fell on Monday, 29 April 2002. We went in for training and we were told not to even bother getting changed because we had to go up to the corporate lounges at the back of the Davie Cooper Stand, where we were all called in one by one and told whether we would be staying or going. I knew I was destined for the chop. It didn't take a rocket scientist to work that one out. I was one of the higher earners, I wasn't playing and the management team were desperate to get rid of me. Andy Dow and I knew we would be amongst the first names on their hit list.

I went in and one of the administration staff told me, 'Your contract is about to be terminated. You will get a severance offer and after you get that you will get X amount in the pound, depending on what the creditors agree on.' That was basically it, and I walked back out again.

It was all done and dusted within minutes, and it really brought a finalisation to everything. I knew it was coming, so at least I was prepared for it, although others were left in a state of shock. It was strange because boys would come out and nod if they had also been sacked or smile if they had been told they were being kept. There were others who were in tears or were so angry that you didn't need them to tell you what they had been told. I have never seen so many differing emotions within one group of people in such a short space of time.

There were loads of security guards on duty at Fir Park that day, and now I can understand why. Emotions run high in tinderbox situations like that, especially when livelihoods are at stake and people are being told they are losing their jobs. Karl Ready was one who lost the plot. He went totally ballistic after he came out of the room. He completely lost it and wanted to take Terry Butcher's head off. Terry had been left as care-taker manager because Eric Black stepped down after the club announced they were going into administration. I think Karl actually tried to go down to the manager's office but didn't get that far because of the security. You could understand Karl's rage, as he had brought his family up from England on prom-ises and his contract from Boyle and his club. We were all treated unfairly and I suppose underneath we all felt the same anger, although some of us kept it hidden a little bit more than others.

We were all wondering how this could have happened if John Boyle had so much money. The administrators tried to explain that it had nothing to do with Boyle, it had been circumstances outwith his control, but none of the boys bought any of that. We all felt he could have done a lot more. I also felt a bit of anger towards Terry Butcher and Chris McCart because of the way they had treated me and Andy Dow in our final few weeks at the club, although I'd guess they'd say they were only following instructions.

I look back on that day now and I genuinely believe it could have been handled a lot better than it was. Things could have been done in a far more dignified manner. People knew the financial position the club were in, and there was no way Motherwell was ever going to get out of it. I think that was unforgivable. It wasn't just the players who were affected, a lot of other people behind the scenes lost their jobs as well, and they never got the same exposure as the players. We are talking about the office girls, cleaners and the kitchen staff. It had an impact on just about everybody at the club.

I felt a bit like a criminal when I walked out of Fir Park that final time with a black bag hanging over my shoulder. Security guards escorted all the players to the dressing room to get their stuff and then showed us out of the ground. It was so over-the-top and so unnecessary for guys who had given their all for the club. It was hard because we didn't get a proper chance to say goodbye to the people and friends who we were leaving behind at the club. It was really sad. Alan MacDonald was handing out our tops and gear. I had become close to Alan, his brother David and Betty Pryde. I had known them for a couple of years and I felt like I was leaving some of my own family behind. There were a lot of the girls and staff in tears. It was just a very emotional day. I also felt for the fans, it must have been hard to know their club was in such a financial state. Yet, the whole thing could have been handled with so much more dignity because so many lives were turned upside down by that administration process.

There weren't many players, certainly not experienced first-team boys, who ended up surviving at Fir Park. I wasn't angry and didn't hold any grudges against the boys who were kept. I had nothing against the likes of James McFadden, Martyn Corrigan or Derek Adams; I was pleased for them. What did annoy me was the way the club ring-fenced their assets and kept the players they wanted to keep, the ones who had a future value that the club could cash in on. That seems to be the case whenever a football team goes into administration. It doesn't seem to come down to what you are earning, it is more a case of what you are worth. If you haven't got a transfer value then you know there is a fair chance that you will get the chop. I would also love to know who decided what boys were staying and going.

I felt I did well during my time at Motherwell. I could have done even better, without a shadow of doubt, but I genuinely felt I made an impact in my time at Fir Park. I was disappointed with the way things had ended. I walked out of the club being owed an awful lot of money, I was probably due about £240,000 from my Motherwell contract. I think initially all we got was 10p in the pound. I think my first cheque was for about £24,000, although I did get some further payments later on. I knew I was never going to get anywhere near what I was due, but a lot of the boys still believed they would get it all. I knew that was very unlikely.

When the club went into administration and my contract was ripped up, I remember thinking to myself, 'What am I going to do now?' I was going to have to sell the house because I had all these loans against it and there would be no money left for Jill or Emma. I also had to come clean with Jill and tell her the truth. Our relationship was already all but over because of my gambling, and I was taking a lot of the frustration at what was happening at the club home with me. It was Jill and Emma who suffered the most. Things weren't great and administration just threw my life into total chaos.

I was suddenly going from a basic of £2,000 a week to absolutely nothing. I had no money and we had to put our house up for sale right away. I had to raise some funds from somewhere. We were lucky because we knew a couple of people who wanted to buy our house, so we didn't even need to put it on the market and that saved some money on estate agent fees. Within six weeks the house was sold and we had moved out of Motherwell. I had nowhere to go because Jill and I had split up, so I ended up going back to stay at my mum and dad's. That at least limited any outgoings.

I had borrowed so much money and secured it against the house. If I could have got away without paying those loans as well then I would have tried, but I had no option because they were all interlinked to the house sale. As soon as it was complete they took their money from the profit. It was so bad that after everything was paid off Jill and I made just £8,000 profit from the house sale. It was a joke because we had sold it for a lot more than we had initially bought it for.

Trying to explain to Jill that that was all the money we had left was hard. I had really let her and Emma down. I still lived on the excuse that I had money coming from Motherwell. I told her that I would give her the money she was due when I got that. I didn't even have the decency to give her any of that £8,000 profit we had made, even though it was Jill's money that had paid the mortgage. I took it to the bookies and I lost it within a couple of days.

When I eventually went to Hearts, a lot of my signing-on fee went to Jill. I gave her roughly the same amount of money she was due. In reality, she was probably due a lot more, but she just wanted enough so she could move on with her life without me. The good thing was that we remained and are still friends today. We obviously had Emma, so that was important. We both moved back to Edinburgh. I was thirty and I was back staying with my parents, but my finances were that bad I had no other option.

A one-time Saint – at my first senior club
St Johnstone.

A top-flight opportunity – helping Raith Rovers to
mix it with Celtic.

Sickening Gazza – celebrating my Raith Rovers goal
against Rangers.

Playing and blowing a ton during my
Morton career.

My Parkhead paradise – celebrating my Motherwell winner as we beat Celtic 1-0.

Scoring the goal against Rangers – in the final day race for UEFA Cup qualification.

My joy soon turns to pain as we beat Rangers and then hear Hearts have pipped us to Europe.

John Spencer and I join some fans to show off the new Motherwell kit.

Very much at home at Fir Park.

Working under Eric Black definitely gave me plenty of food for thought.

My boyhood dream turns into a nightmare at Hearts.

The *Daily Star* breaks the heartbreaking news that Motherwell are set for administration.

The day me and the rest of my Motherwell teammates were sacked.

I speak to teammate Stevie Nicholas and my co-author Scott Burns after I leave Fir Park for the last time.

Eddie Forrest and I get our first cheques from the Motherwell administrators.

The Danderhall Bowling club team who won the 2008 Scotland Top Ten competition.

The Scottish pool team at the 2012 European Championships.

I pop the champagne as Whitehill Welfare lift the 2012 League Cup.

Life's a beach – Jac and I on Musselburgh Beach on our wedding day.

Jac and I cut our wedding cake.

Mum, Dad, my sister Nicola and my niece, Kelsa join Jac and I to celebrate our wedding.

My best men – Craig Dargo and Elliot Smith – flank me on my big day.

A team game – my former Motherwell teammates Andy Goram, Shaun Fagan and Don Goodman join in the celebrations.

My tower of strength – Jac and I after I proposed in Blackpool.

My Nana and Granny Twaddle.

Future generations – Emma with my grandson, Jack.

Brush strokes –
back on the tools.

Arthur gives me my pin at Gamblers Anonymous.

A lot of lives and careers were devastated by administration at Motherwell. I was lucky football-wise because I knew there was interest in me from Sheffield United and Hearts. Some of my teammates, though, weren't so fortunate. Their careers were left in tatters. Careers were ended and it is cruel when a dream is crushed the way it was for some of my Motherwell teammates. It was also at a time when there wasn't a lot of money in Scottish football. The major television deal had just collapsed and contracts were few and far between. Karl Ready, Eddie Forrest, Stevie Nicholas and Mark Brown all had to go down the way. Mark Brown did manage to work his way back up at Inverness and got his move to Celtic and then Hibs, but things didn't work out so well for the rest of the boys. Stevie and Eddie had to drop down the leagues. They had to get full-time jobs, but credit to them, they are still playing today. The biggest fall was probably Karl. He arrived in Scotland as a Welsh international defender but after he was sacked he ended up at Aldershot Town, Aylesbury United, Crawley Town and Farnborough. It is fair to say the big man was one of the unlucky ones, as his career never really recovered.

Losing jobs at Motherwell took a lot of the joy and excitement out of the game for so many. It was hardly surprising, as you think you have a contract and suddenly it is ripped up and you are left with almost nothing. It is always going to have an impact, no matter what level you are playing at.

The thing that really annoyed me about the whole process at Motherwell was John Boyle and the way he handled the whole situation. He is no longer the chairman and now the club has progressed, but I think there will always be some bitterness to him from the players and staff who were thrown on the scrapheap. People had moved and relocated their families in good faith because they believed that Boyle and his club had given them contracts that would be fulfilled. If things had been so bad, then surely he must have known? So why would you then go ahead and let people make such big changes in their lives? Andy Dow was the prime example. He went and bought a big new house in Carfin and took his wife and family down from Aberdeen. For me, it's just not right that people can do things like that, move families, buy houses and then get left in such a mess through no fault of their own.

A few years later, Boyle went on Sky Sports News to complain about Cardiff City because they had been late in paying part of Paul Quinn's transfer fee. This was the same individual whose decisions got nineteen players and numerous other staff sacked when he put Motherwell into administration. That allowed the club to get rid of our contracts that he had rubber-stamped at a fraction of the money we should have been paid. So that day when he went on Sky Sports News to complain about not getting paid on time was really galling for me, and it smacked of hypocrisy. I could have smashed the television as I watched him take the moral high ground. I thought, 'Who are you to talk about the way other teams handle themselves after what happened at Motherwell?' It wasn't just footballers, it was the club in general he dragged down. I have seen very little remorse from Boyle. I also think it was wrong that Motherwell came out of administration and Boyle was allowed to return as chairman again. That was out of order and just rubbed salt in the wounds of all the people the club had sacked.

I spoke to a few of the boys, like Eddie Forrest and Stevie Nicholas, and they were of the same opinion as me. Eddie will moan about it until the end of his days. I was probably as bitter as Eddie, but now I have moved on. I knew we were never going to get all the money we were owed. I accepted that and just had to try and get what I could out of what was a very difficult situation. A few of the boys still hold on to the hope they will get the rest of their money, but I don't think that is ever going to happen.

I now run my own business and I know how hard it can be. I see so many small businesses go to the wall every year. I have seen a lot of people shut down businesses and start up under a different name just so they can try and clear some of their debts. Boyle, it seems to me, pulled off something similar with administration, and I believe it is morally wrong that people can legally do that. Was he really down to his last pound or penny?

I never really had much contact with Boyle when I was a player at Motherwell. He was very flamboyant and he used to come on the pitch at the end to greet the players if we got a big win. He certainly thought he was important, but he never really was in the dressing room. The only other time we would hear from him was when he offered us extra bonuses if we were to beat either side of the Old Firm, although that happens at a lot of clubs. It was good at Motherwell because initially we had a very good team and we always fancied our chances. If we did beat the Old Firm then we knew we would get another £1,000 in our wage packet.

The other main frustration I have is that so many people at Motherwell went through so much heartbreak and misery, and for what? I just wish Scottish football could have learned from it. We went through a lot and it shouldn't have been for nothing. Since Motherwell, a lot of other clubs have gone into administration. We have had Livingston, Dundee twice, Gretna, who have gone out of business, and the biggest one, obviously, is Rangers. It was bad enough when a club the size of Motherwell went down that road but Rangers are one of the biggest clubs in the world. For a team the size and stature of Rangers it shouldn't be allowed to happen, although it should never be allowed to happen to any club. The football authorities in Scotland need to do so much more to make sure clubs live within their means and stop gambling with hundreds of years of history.

I still have loads of respect for the people behind the scenes at Motherwell. Without question, it was the best place I played during my career. The way I was treated by the fans and so many special people at the club. There were so many special people at the club but sadly a few of them, including Betty Pryde, are no longer with us. I was really sad when she passed away because she was a fantastic person and she did so much for me during my time at Fir Park.

In the end, we all have had to move on. The club spent outwith its means. It is something I have done in my own life and so I can't say too much on that front. That is life, and you just have to get on with things. I still have fond memories from my time at Motherwell. I still have a lot of time for the club and the fans, and I always enjoy going back to Fir Park and that will always remain the case.

14

MY HEART'S NOT IN IT

Trawling through the wreckage of administration was difficult. I knew I had to dust myself down and try to find another club. I wasn't bringing any money in, but that didn't stop me from spending what I didn't have. I stole. I was involved in fraud and taking money from people that I shouldn't have been anywhere near. I look back at some of the characters I was in contact with and I wouldn't have the bottle to go anywhere near them today. I was absolutely mad. I knew I was endangering my own life, but I couldn't have cared less. I just wanted money and I didn't care where it came from. I didn't worry about the consequences.

I was still mad on casinos, dogs, horses and football. Most of my money went down those avenues, although there were also new emerging markets that started to reel me in. I began piling money on virtual horse racing. I was never one for computer games or consoles, but I got hooked on betting virtual horses running across a screen. I also started to play the virtual roulette machines that the bookies started to take in.

The roulette machines in particular can absolutely destroy you. I have seen it happen. It is so easy for people to get hooked on them and to lose big money. I used to think, 'Why do the bookies stay open even when all the horses and dog races were finished?' It is because of these virtual machines. I was recently told how much the bookies make from these machines, and the figures are absolutely staggering. They make millions. They coin in as much from them as they do dog, horse or football betting. I thought it was great because I could gamble from the second I walked into a bookies until the second the shop was locked up. My betting was non-stop, it was relentless, but now you can bet twenty-four hours a day, seven days a week. I hate to think what would have happened to me if that had been the case in my betting prime. I had big enough debts that I knew I would eventually have to pay back, but I was always confident that I would get a new club and I could use some of my next signing-on fee to clear my feet.

I knew Hearts were interested in me and I could also have gone to Sheffield United. I knew I had an escape route. That is where I was lucky in my football career. There are times when I did get big lump sums and that always bailed me out. I knew I was still more than capable of earning a fair bit of money through my football. The Hearts manager Craig Levein phoned and spoke to me after Motherwell had gone into administration. He told me money was tight, but he was interested in signing me. He couldn't guarantee me anything but he was confident they could put a deal together to take me to Tynecastle that summer. At that point, I also knew there was concrete interest from Sheffield United. My former Motherwell teammate David Kelly had told me and then I had spoken to their manager Neil Warnock. I knew he wanted to sign me. He had tried to get me several times previously. I was getting a bit jumpy because I didn't want to say no to Sheffield United and be left with nothing. Hearts were my boyhood team and my preference, but I needed to know there was definitely going to be something there.

I went down to Sheffield for a couple of days to look around Bramall Lane and to meet Warnock and his assistant Kevin

Blackwell. I spent the first day with Neil and the Warnock family. They couldn't have been more welcoming. The next day my agent came down and started to discuss terms. I knew when I was sitting there that I had no intention of signing. I didn't even know why I was there wasting everybody's time. If Hearts were going to deal me in then it didn't matter how much Sheffield United were going to offer me.

It also made my life a little easier knowing that I was staying in Scotland. I had my issues, my nana was dying and my mum also wasn't well. My life was complicated enough without having to drag myself away from Scotland. Looking back, what an opportunity I let slip away. Warnock sold United to me as if I was Lionel Messi. He told me how the United fans loved tricky wingers and I could become the darling of Bramall Lane. He walked me round the ground and he pointed to the big stand behind one of the goals and said, 'This is where the fans go ballistic.' But it didn't matter to me. He even pushed the boat out for me. He offered me a two-year contract with a massive signing-on fee and a relocation package, but I still walked away from it all.

I knew at that point I was going to get an offer from Hearts. They tabled a one-year deal on a fraction of the money that Sheffield United had offered. If you looked at both contracts side by side, United should have been a no-brainer, but not for me. I signed for Hearts.

I went to Hearts because I was a fan but it was also my next place of employment that would provide me with a regular income which would allow me to bet. I also got a signing-on fee and I needed that to get out of a massive financial hole. Craig Levein wasn't too far behind Mr Warnock with his sales pitch either. He told me that I was coming to Hearts as one of his main signings of that summer, I was coming with a big reputation and people knew I was a big player in the Scottish game. He also said that, being a Jambo, he knew the fans would get right behind me. It should have been a dream move for both us.

It was funny because Craig was one of the stars of the Hearts team I followed when I was younger. As with every other Hearts fan, the 1985–86 season is one I will never forget. I was at Dens Park, Dundee, on that tear-filled day that was 3 May 1986. I had gone up with my dad on the Prestonpans Hearts bus that used to leave Danderhall every second week. It was an afternoon where I finally hoped Hearts would win the title, but it ended in total devastation for everybody in maroon and white. I remember sitting at the side of the road crying after the match. I was absolutely crestfallen when we lost to Dundee and Celtic beat St Mirren to pip us and leave us with nothing but final day heartbreak.

I never missed the football before I started playing. Most of the time I went to gamble, although I still had feelings for Hearts, and what happened over the course of that week, was – if you pardon the pun – heartbreaking. I remember when Albert Kidd scored his second goal, the windows in the Dens Park office got put in. I ended up sitting on the kerb after the game, and I was just in absolute bits. Maybe things would have been different if Craig Levein had been fit for that that game at Dens. Who knows?

I was also at Hampden for the Scottish Cup final against Aberdeen the week after. Things didn't get any better. I was late, and by the time I had got to the national stadium we were already getting beat. I think we were always going to lose after what had happened at Dens Park. It was even harder for the Hearts fans to take because I don't think the club will come so close to winning a League and Cup double again.

I at least had the chance to try and bring some success to Tynecastle, but I think back to that period and I have to say I don't know if I really had any great interest in playing football. That is the God-honest truth. I look back now, and I was in a hole. I knew my football career was down to the final few years. My interest in the game had also severely waned after the way things had ended for me at Fir Park. There had been the administration process and also my gambling. Everything had worn me down and squeezed the joy of playing football right out of me. I think if I had been offered another job on the same money then I would probably have taken it. I no longer had the buzz, and I wasn't really interested in the flash life of being a footballer. I didn't want to attract attention; I just wanted to sneak about in the shadows, betting my life away, without anybody noticing.

I recall being out on the Tynecastle pitch the day I signed holding a Hearts top. It was the day I had waited all my life for, but did I really want to be there? I don't know if I really did. Did I want to be at Hearts? Probably not. It was just another vice to get me out of a lot of financial trouble caused by gambling. I got a lot of money for signing on at Hearts, and that was another big attraction. I loved my time at St Johnstone, Raith, Morton and Motherwell, although my gambling grew steadily worse with every move.

I know walking into Tynecastle with that carefree attitude was hardly ideal. I hoped my outlook would change when the games started and I got to meet all the lads, but it didn't. We went out on our pre-season to Finland and things turned into a nightmare from the very start. I played in our first game. I did okay and put in some good early crosses. Everything was going well until I went to take a corner, and as soon as I kicked the ball, I felt my thigh go. I had torn my thigh muscle and I ended up with an inch and a half tear down it. I knew that was me, and I would be out for several weeks. I was always going to be struggling for the first few games of the season. That only added to the many negative thoughts going round in my head, and it meant I was going into another campaign without a pre-season. I was mentally gone and physically struggling, so how was my move to Hearts ever going to work? I was scrambled.

I no longer wanted to get away from defenders; I was more interested in keeping away from debt collectors. I quickly gambled away my signing-on fee from Hearts and took out more loans and credit cards. That was a road I had never gone down before. I was in a real financial mess, even though I was earning more than £2,000 a week, with appearance money and good bonuses on top of that. It was just spend, spend, spend. My head wasn't on football. I was just sick with gambling.

There was a boy, Richard Cunningham, whom I went to college with. He was a really close friend and he was absolutely delighted when I went to Tynecastle because he was a big Hearts fan. I took advantage of him and borrowed money from him, and I didn't even attempt to pay that back. It got to the point where I couldn't even afford to repay him. He was ready to come in to the club to make sure he got his money. Eventually, my mum and dad had to give him what he was owed. This was a guy who tried to help me, gave me money in good faith, and I just treated him with total contempt. That is sore, because he is a really good lad.

I know my attitude at times was far from ideal, but I certainly wasn't the only person like that at Hearts. Alan Rae was the physiotherapist and I thought his attitude towards me was terrible. He had his favourites and if you weren't one of them then it was a case of 'tough'. I thought the way he spoke to some of the staff and players was totally out of order. I had already torn my thigh in Finland and things hadn't gone great. For me, seeing him every day to get treatment was far from ideal – and

I think it's fair to say we never saw eye to eye. I don't know if he was aware of some of the rubbish that was going on in my life or not, but I knew I was never going to really get on with him.

I hardly did any training at all when I returned from Finland because of that early thigh tear, but the manager still put me on the bench for the start of the season. He was just desperate for me to play and be involved as I was one of his main signings. I came off the bench to make my debut in that opening day against Dundee. To be fair to the Hearts fans, I came on to a great reception, knowing I was a Jambo. I came on as a substitute again in our next match. That was my first taste of the Edinburgh derby as a player, and what a day it was for every Hearts fan. Big Mark de Vries was the hero. Mark is a fantastic guy and I still keep in touch with him now. He is a lovely big man and he did a fantastic job for Hearts when he was there. He came in and was an overnight sensation. He will always go down in Tynecastle folklore for scoring the four goals in that amazing 5–1 win over the Hibees. I also picked up an injury in that game that I will go into more detail about in the next chapter.

After three or four games, I knew things weren't great. It should have been a dream come true, but in all honesty, it was torture. I had never expected it to be like that. I just wasn't enjoying it. I wasn't training or playing well. I had fallen out of love with football. My life was in total turmoil because of my gambling, but nobody at the club knew anything about that.

The only time anybody at Hearts got the slightest hint of my problem was when sheriff officers arrived at the stadium to serve me with a summons because I had reneged on one of my loans – where I had owed a substantial five-figure sum. I had to go out and speak to these two men who served me with a warrant and told me I had to clear my debt within weeks or I would be going to court. It was a real embarrassment to the girls in the office, for the manager and the football club. I then had to go in and see Craig Levein and explain to him why they had been there. I was so stupid. I had the chance to get help, but I just brushed it off with a 'that's life' attitude. When the sheriff officers came in, the manager pulled me aside and asked me what was going on. I just played things down, brushed them away. I said it was something that had happened previously, but I don't know if he believed me or not.

That was the one and only time that the sheriff's officers turned up at Tynecastle, but they were never far away from my parents' front door. I had also started to build up massive debts with one of the players at the club. He had his own betting account, and I used to put thousands on through him. Like everything else in my life at the stage, it was a costly affair.

I was in a world of my own, in my own little bubble, when I was at Hearts. That is the only way I can describe the situation I was in. It was just a bizarre place to be in, especially at a club that I had supported all my days and had travelled all across Europe to watch. Every Hearts fans would have loved to have been in my boots. A few years earlier, I might have felt the same, but gambling had just completely killed me as a person. I was in a relationship and I had settled down for a bit, but that was only a temporary measure. I was soon back to living a lie. I was living two separate lives. I was showing up to work as a footballer, but away from Tynecastle I was a manic gambler. I never had any money left. Every time I got paid, it would be immediately blown away. I was living two lives and neither of them brought much happiness.

15

NANA'S TALE

I loved my nana, Annie Barker, to bits. I really did. When she died I was in a dark, dark place. Shamefully, it wasn't in grief or sorrow, it was down to my gambling. I went round to her house every other day to see her in those final few months. Yes, it was to see if she was okay, but that wasn't my primary objective. I went round to visit her because I knew she had money and I needed it to gamble. I basically stole from her so I could bet. I live with that guilt every day. I feel really terrible that somebody, her own flesh and blood, could stoop so low. You may find hard to believe, but this was someone I loved and I was really close to, someone who meant the world to me. I know I had a funny way of showing it.

My nana was dying when I was at Motherwell, and she finally passed away by the time I had moved to Hearts. She was in her eighties and she wasn't well. She was falling out of the bed and was in and out of hospital. She had bad arthritis, and I knew she wasn't doing great. When I was at Motherwell, she was really struggling. I used to travel through to see her most days, and I would go down to her house to sit with her for a wee bit and then tuck her in before she went to sleep. I would then go back up to stay at my mum and dad's. I would then get a lift back through with the Motherwell chief executive Pat Nevin the next morning. My mum used to say what a great laddie I was because it looked like I was doing so much for my nana.

I did love my nana dearly, but I also had another sick reason for those regular visits to her house. I saw her as a way of funding my gambling habit. She had a box in the living room where she kept all her money, probably the crux of what she had saved up through her life. I got a key cut for it and basically stole all her life savings out of it. I didn't go into the box and take all the money in one swoop, but gradually over the months I took out small amounts until there was next to nothing left. I don't know how much money I actually stole from her. I would hate to know what the exact figure was. It was a substantial amount and at a guess I would say it would have been in excess of £10,000, if I am being totally honest. What sort of person would do that to their own nana? There are no words that can describe the shame I feel. I don't say that for sympathy because after the way I treated my nana that is the last thing I should be entitled to. The most galling thing is that if I had just asked my nana for the money I know she would have happily given it to me, but I didn't want to tell anyone I had a gambling problem.

I watched my nana die, and I have to be honest, I know it might sound cold-hearted, and it was, but I didn't even want to go to her funeral. Not because I didn't love her or I was unable to cope with the grief, but because I had an illness. I was caught up in a gambling frenzy. To most people who maybe haven't had a betting addiction, it might sound like a load of rubbish, a cock-and-bull story to try and justify my actions, but it wasn't. I don't think any sane individual could defend my actions. But when you are a gambling addict, it consumes you and takes over your life without you even knowing. It is hard to explain. It is like a computer virus. It might start off as a small thing, but it spreads quickly and often causes irreparable damage from within. Gambling becomes all-consuming; it becomes the be-all and end-all. You will go to extreme lengths and measures just so you can put on a bet and satisfy your cravings and impulses. I was that sick, although I didn't even realise it.

My nana died on 24 November 2003. I didn't want to grieve. The only place I wanted to be was at the bookies. I wasn't thinking that I had lost my nana. I wasn't really that bothered that my mum had lost her mother or my sister had lost her nana. I wasn't thinking about anyone but myself. Her funeral even spoiled my day, not because I had lost her but because it kept me out of the bookies. I know it sounds terrible, and it was, but that is what an illness like gambling can do to you. I had maybe only missed a few dog races that morning, but it still left me in a foul mood. I even left my nana's funeral early so I could get to the book-makers for the first horse race of the day. That was all that mattered to me. It was the highlight of my day, even when my nana was laid to rest.

I look back on that day with nothing but shame and embar-rassment. How could I have done that to somebody I was so close to? How sick was that? There can be no excuses, even though I was in such a bad place with gambling. It had taken over my life and was at the centre of everything I did. Thinking back I am just relieved I went to the funeral because I wouldn't have been able to live with myself if I hadn't gone and prob-ably back then it would have been touch and go. I should have been the first person there because my nana did so much for me and was one of the most caring and loving people I ever met.

What I did to my nana was absolutely despicable and inex-cusable. It will become even more so when I tell you everything she did for me. My nana was like a second mum to me when I was younger. I spent so much time with my nana at her house when I was growing up. I was really close to her and she was so good to me. When it came to birthdays and Christmases, she would spoil me rotten. She would always buy me brilliant presents and stuff that I had always wanted and harked on about for weeks.

When I stayed at home I pretty much saw my nana every day. When I was still at school I would go round every morning for breakfast. She was a big part of my life. My nana was also so close to my mum, and we all used to spend a lot of time together. I remember she used to take me for walks. My mum used to work and so I would go round to my nana's to stay until my mum or dad had finished their work. She was so kind and generous, and I know she would have done absolutely anything for me. That is why it makes the things I have done to her even more galling. I wish I could turn back time, I really do, but I can't and it is something I will have to live with for the rest of my days.

Even when I was playing football I never gave her anything. I gave all my tops and boots away. The only things I have left from my career are the scrapbooks my mum and dad kept for me and a DVD of all my goals. If it hadn't been for my parents keeping those things, then I would have nothing from my football career outwith my memories. The problem was I didn't actually give my family a second thought. I should have given them a top or boots, but I didn't. They were the ones who were giving me and they got next to nothing back in return.

I know how proud my nana was of my football career. She used to watch every football show on the television to see if she could see me playing or maybe doing an interview. She watched the football programmes constantly, whether it was the local news, *Sportscene* or *Scotsport*, in case I was on it. I know how much it meant to her. When I had scored or done well I used to phone her or go round and tell her how I had got on. She would then ask if I had done any interviews, and if I had, she would either get the papers or wait patiently to see my goal or interviews on the television. If I had been on television then the phone would go a few minutes after and it would be my nana to say she was so proud of me.

I know she worked hard to get everything she had. She was riddled with arthritis and in pain in her final few years. Yet she battled through it every day and was always there to offer love, help and advice whenever any of her family or friends needed it. It is not as if she had an easy life, either. She lost her husband, John Peacock, quite early on in a road accident. I wasn't even born, so unfortunately I didn't even get to meet my grandad.

I had my gran, Annie Twaddle, and my papa, Willie Twaddle, on my dad's side. My papa also used to come and watch all my football and would bring my dog, Sheba, with him. I used to take the dog everywhere but I wouldn't always come back with it. I would take the dog to the bookies and then I would come out and forget about her because I was so engrossed in my gambling. I would walk home and my mum would ask me, 'Where is Sheba?'

I would reply, 'I don't know.' I would then troop back round to the bookies and poor Sheba would still be sitting there outside, in all conditions. My papa would have to save Sheba half the time and go and get her. He would look after her and take her on long walks that were far more exciting than going up the High Street to Coral's, Ladbrokes or William Hill.

I loved all my grandparents, but it was my nana and my Auntie Margaret who were the two people I looked up to the most. They were both really, really special people to me. My auntie was my nana's sister, and I got on really well with her and my Uncle John. She died of leukaemia, and I was absolutely devastated when she passed away.

My Auntie Margaret was pretty well off and I used to get money off her all the time. Unknown to her, she ended up funding a lot of my gambling. I was a very manipulative person. I used to lie and con her just to get money from her. I used to tell her all sorts of rubbish like I needed money to get my mum stuff or my mum was struggling for cash that particular week. I stole an awful lot of money off her through my dishonest ways, although I never physically stole the money off her. I never went and took money off her without asking for it first.

I think, at the end, my nana knew about my gambling, although, like everybody else, she didn't know the full extent of it. I did some horrible things to her, but I do genuinely miss her terribly and I do think about her every day. I just wish she were still here to see me today. I just hope that if she is looking down on me that maybe she can be proud of the person I am now. I am a very different one to who waved her farewell from this world.

I will also tell you a rather quirky Nana story. I am now with my wife Jac, but before we met, my nana, mum, sister and I used to go to Burntisland in Fife every year for a day out. My nana used to love it the older she got. She would sit and play the slot machines. I would sit next to her – surprise, surprise – and at the same time I would also feed my own addiction. We then would have a picnic or maybe go for fish and chips. It was a real family day out. We did it all the time.

The ironic thing is that Jac's nana, Janet Peggs, who I became really close to before she died, actually stayed in Burntisland, in one of the streets we used to walk up after we came off the train from Edinburgh. Some people might think it is coincidence, but I believe in karma. For me, that is more fate than coincidence. We had passed her nana's house ever year.

Thankfully, by the time I had met Jac and her nana, I had stopped gambling. I became really close to Jac's nana. She was also a really lovely person and I think I also saw a bit of my own nana in her. I had learned my lesson and I felt I had been given a second chance. I treated Jac's nana the way I should have treated my own. Jac's nana died in 2010, and I took it really hard because a bit of my nana also went with her. It was a big loss. It was demoralising and hard. It felt like I had lost my own nana all over again.

16

LOSING IT AT BREAK-NECK SPEED

At times, the football would be an escape from my gambling problem, but when my luck was out, it was well and truly out. The derby trouncing of Hibs may have been the highlight of the 2002–03 season for every Hearts fan, but that match turned out to be the beginning of the end of my Tynecastle career.

During that match, I suffered a hefty blow to the neck, from which I have never fully recovered. It was more a clumsy accident than anything else. I was waiting for the ball to come out of the air and saw the Hibs striker Paco Luna behind me, but I knew there was no chance of him getting to the ball. I didn't think there was any problem until the Spaniard came crashing into the back of me, landing on my neck. Right away I was in agony, the pain was so excruciating. I knew I had done myself damage, but I was hoping it was nothing too serious. I was sent for an X-ray after the game, but nothing showed up. I tried to shrug it off but I knew my injury was going to be a lot more complicated. I went home that night and despite the 5–1 win, I wasn't in the mood to celebrate. I could hardly sleep and every time I moved my neck I was in bits. I didn't sleep a wink that night.

I got up early the next morning and got a lift to Tynecastle. I went and saw the physio, Alan Rae, and told him there was something seriously wrong with my neck. I was in absolute agony;

the pain was intolerable. I had never experienced anything like it in my life before. Alan didn't seem overly concerned, presumably because the X-ray hadn't picked anything up, and told me that he thought I maybe had a touch of whiplash. He said my neck should settle down, but if I was still in as much pain the following day, he would arrange to get it looked at.

Assuming it wasn't too serious, he gave me strengthening workouts for my neck. I did a session of these exercises, although he obviously had no idea at this point that I had a far more serious problem. It will come as no surprise to know that I was still in absolute agony on the Sunday evening when I returned home. I just knew there was something wrong with my back or the top of my neck. I could hardly move it and I knew that wasn't right.

I went back to Tynecastle to see Alan on the Monday and he sent me up to get a scan on my neck. It revealed I had prolapsed my C5 and C6 discs in my neck. In a nutshell, I had basically broken my neck. I was told that I would need neurosurgery to get back to full fitness. I couldn't believe it when I was told the news. It was a long way from nothing showing up on an X-ray to possible whiplash to needing a potentially life-threatening operation and it came as more than a bit of a shock. I found it hard to believe what was happening.

My neck was absolutely knackered. I had to wait a couple of weeks before I could get my operation because the specialist, who was the only woman in Scotland at the time who performed the surgery, was away. If I wanted to get the operation any earlier then I would have had to have gone down to England, but I knew I wouldn't have had any family or friends round me.

The consultant told me the ins and outs of the operation and that there was a very high risk to the procedure. She said there was a 25 to 30 percent chance that I could end up paralysed. She explained how she would have to open up the opposite side of my throat to get through to the other side of my neck. I was told if they went through the area I had damaged then there would have been even more risk of me being left paralysed because there are 75 percent more nerves on the right-hand side than your left. I waited and had the operation at the Western Infirmary in Edinburgh. I went through neurosurgery for six hours. It was a big operation. They had to put a cage round my neck and insert six pins and four screws to support it.

That is the only major operation I have had in my life and it was absolutely horrendous, although I have to say a huge thank you to the surgeon and all her staff for doing such a good job. I was told that they might need to leave some tubes in my neck after the operation to try and flush some of the bruised blood away. When I came around I actually thought I was still halfway through the surgery because I felt my neck and there were no tubes sticking out, but the nurse said that things had gone well and they hadn't needed to leave the tubes in. I spent the next week on a morphine drip because of the pain. Half the time I didn't even know I had visitors because I was so doped up and out of things.

The only blessing from that was that it stopped me from gambling temporarily. I had nowhere to bet and I was away from the everyday temptations. There was also a Hearts team-mate who I owed money to and I was able to avoid the constant pressure and demands of him trying to get the money I owed.

I eventually got out of the Western and I was sent up to Murrayfield Hospital, where I spent another couple of weeks convalescing. The thing that annoyed me more than anything else was that I hardly had any contact with the club. Nobody came in to see if I was okay, apart from my girlfriend, my family, my friends and some of the younger boys from Hearts, like Elliott Smith.

When I came out of hospital I was told to take it easy. I went every couple of days to see the physio, but I never saw many of the boys because I wasn't training. I hadn't been a big fan of the physio before my injury, and after it that situation certainly didn't improve. He was a physio, but I always thought that he considered himself to be more than that. He always seemed to have an opinion on everything. You would listen to him and at times he would even be trying to talk tactics with the boys.

At the time I was also disappointed with the way the physio had dealt with my injury. I thought that he should have listened to me more, then he might have realised that my neck problem really was serious despite the X-ray. I know that none of us can get things right all the time, but what happened with that neck injury did nothing to help our relationship. Looking back, I think me and him just didn't get on but I'm sure he did his best for me at the time. It was just one of those things.

I spent a lot of time on my own and away from the ground as I tried to get back to near normality, before I could even think about kicking a ball again. It left me gambling like daft again. I was still in massive debt and so my situation was only ever going to get worse. I owed thousands to this first-team player at Hearts who put hundreds of phone bets on for me. I couldn't put any more bets on with him and that was when I started stealing more from my family. I was also taking money from people I shouldn't have been, but I knew I always had a way out. My debts were increasing, but I always had it at the back of my mind that I would get my money from Motherwell and then I would be able to pay everyone off. I knew I was going to get a fair amount. I didn't know how much because we were still waiting to see how much in the pound the administrators

131

were going to give us. I certainly knew it would be a big cheque because the first one is normally the main one in these circumstances. So I wasn't really that bothered about my situation. I felt I could come out on top. I was also putting on weight because I couldn't do anything and I was no longer training. I was hardly in the ideal place to be a professional footballer.

I knew there was a fair idea that I wasn't going to play again until the end of the season. My contract was also up and so I knew the odds, as always, were firmly stacked against me getting a new deal. I got the all-clear to get back two or three weeks before the end of the season. The specialist carried out several different checks on my neck, and I was told everything was going to be fine and I could go back training. I went back and I actually thought I wanted to try and do everything in my power to get another contract at Hearts. I believed there might be a wee chance that I could win a new deal, even if it was on vastly reduced terms. That hope gave me with a wee chink of light, although I still don't know why. I approached those last couple of weeks like I was on trial. I went out and gave my all, but it counted for next to nothing.

The manager pulled me in and said I wasn't being offered another contract. He told me things hadn't gone the way either of us had hoped and it would be best for both of us to go in different directions. I wasn't surprised and I completely understand why Craig Levein didn't offer me a new deal. We parted on really good terms and the manager wished me all the best. We shook hands and I walked out.

I have a lot of time for Craig. He is a top coach and manager. He was a bit of a disciplinarian, but he had a good attitude and he loved his boys. He had the respect of everyone at the club and most people within football. It is hardly a surprise that he has done so well in the game. He left Hearts to go to Leicester, although things didn't really work out for him down there. Obviously, Leicester are a big club but he went there at a difficult time financially and that was probably the biggest factor as to why Craig wasn't as successful down there as he should have been. He has since come back up and made his name with Dundee United and is now the Scotland manager. He has really taken the country forward, and I firmly believe that if he is not head-hunted before then, that he can lead us back to the finals of either a World Cup or the European Championships.

If it had been any other period in my life then it probably would have been a career highlight and a happy time playing for Hearts, but because of my circumstances, it wasn't. If it had been the start of my playing days then things might have been different, but it wasn't. I was in such a state with my gambling and it was a really dark period for me. People say to me it must have been great to play in the derby and for Hearts, but it wasn't. If I look back on my career, I don't actually see myself as a Hearts player. When you tell people that, especially Hearts fans, they are amazed. They always say it must have been great to have been involved in that 5–1 derby win. As far as I am concerned, I never achieved anything at Hearts when I was there. Absolutely nothing. I never gave anything like I should have. Gambling played a big part in that, although the injury certainly didn't help me either. That was a once in a lifetime opportunity and I never took it. All I did was pick up a wage for a year and basically let Craig Levein down. I really felt for Craig because I just didn't do it for him. He had put a lot of faith in me. He expected a lot more than he actually ended up getting.

The good thing from my time at Hearts was that I made a lot of good friends. I got on well with Steven Boyack, Mark de Vries, Jean-Louis Valois, Roddy McKenzie, Austin McCann and Stephen Simmons. I still keep in touch with them all. There is also Neil

Janczyk and Elliott Smith, who was one of the best men at my wedding, along with Craig Dargo. I still have a lot of friends there. Another Hearts player I have to give a big mention to is Steven Pressley. I don't know if he ever knew how bad my gambling was, although I think he might have.

When he was at Hearts he put me in one of his flats in Stockbridge and he never took any money off me. It was an empty flat, and he could have quite easily charged me rent but he never asked me for a penny. I just got the feeling he knew I was in dire straits, although he never ever mentioned my personal life or things away from football. I had and still have a lot of respect for 'Elvis'. He wasn't your stereotypical footballer. He was very articulate, clever and very different from most other professionals. He was also a genuinely nice guy and he helped me whenever he could. I now see him as a manager, and I am not surprised he is doing so well. As a captain, he was a real leader and an inspiration to those around him. He was also a really big family guy. He started out managing at Falkirk, and I am sure he will to go on and manage at the very highest level. I am in absolutely no doubt about that because he has all the attributes you need to be a top manager.

It was at that point – leaving Hearts – there was the realisation that I was completely knackered. My professional football career was now over. I had this cheque coming from Motherwell, but I also knew I would need to find another job. I felt there was no chance of anybody else signing me because of my neck and the fact I had hardly kicked a ball for Hearts. Where could I go from here?

17

BRASS-NECKING IT FROM
LOVE STREET TO CIVVY STREET

I had left Hearts and it was a case of, 'Well, what am I going to do now?' I knew my neck was unlikely to stand up to the daily rigours of professional football, and secondly, who was going to offer me a contract? I knew that if my phone was going to ring then it was going to be a debt collector rather than a football manager looking for an ageing winger who had still to prove that he could overcome major neck surgery.

I was considering my options away from the game, although I have to say for an addicted gambler none of them looked too appealing or offered anywhere near the money I had become accustomed to at both Motherwell and Hearts. Nothing stood out or was going to help me even put a dent in my mountain of debts, not that I was really bothered about that, because any money I could lay my hands on was going to be gambled. That was a cast-iron certainty.

I was getting all set for Civvy Street and maybe a long overdue dose of reality when my mobile did ring. I got the shock of my life when I took the call and it was the St Mirren manager John Coughlin. He wanted to know if I would be interested in moving to the Buddies. They were in the First Division at the time, although John had ambitions of leading them back into the

Scottish Premier League. He had been the assistant to Tom Hendrie when they had last been in the top flight and was keen to get a crack at the SPL in his own right.

He explained he wanted me to bring a bit of width and flair to his team. He asked me how I was and how my fitness was after the neurosurgery. Was I completely honest? Probably not. I certainly didn't feel 100 percent, and the neurosurgery had left me in absolute bits. I knew I had no chance of getting anywhere near the levels I had set at some of my previous clubs. I just hoped I could get by and show some fleeting glimpses of my old self. I quickly agreed terms with John and I knew it was too good an opportunity to turn down. I was also offered a good financial package by First Division standards, and, coming from Hearts, probably gave me a bit more financial leverage when it came to those negotiations.

If I am being honest, I only signed on at St Mirren for the money, nothing else. I had no real interest in travelling from Edinburgh to Paisley every day. I only went to St Mirren for cash. I saw it as a way of making easy money. It was wrong and it is certainly not a decision from my football career that I am proud of.

When you have been through neurosurgery there is a fair chance you will struggle with neurosis, when you get pains in other bits of your body that come from where you have had your neck surgery. I was getting that in my back and legs. I knew within a couple of days' travelling that I had made a bad mistake in signing for St Mirren. I started to have really bad problems with my back. I was in bits, and even now I still get a lot of bother from it. I spent half my time in Paisley on the physio's table because I just wasn't up to it. I was kidding everyone on, including myself.

The only real highlight from my time at St Mirren was the fact that I finally got that first cheque from Motherwell. I had to use that money to pay off the money I was due to my former Hearts teammate. He had to wait months for his cash, as I had expected to get my money from Motherwell well before I did. The day my cheque cleared I had to phone up the bank so I could get the money, which was thousands, so I could finally pay him off. I then continued on my pursuit to see how quickly I could lose the rest of it. I had promised to put that first payment towards a deposit for a flat with an ex-girlfriend, but I never put a penny anywhere near it. I still had thousands of pounds of debt, but apart from the Hearts player and Jill, who was given some of the money she was owed, I never paid anyone else off. I just went and gambled the rest away in a matter of days.

St Mirren had also gambled in signing me, and it was clear from very early on that it wasn't one that was about to see them come up trumps. I went there and I only played three games. I made one start and two substitutes appearances in the league. I would have liked to have done better, but I just wasn't fit. I was no longer up to the level required to be a professional footballer. Even in the games I did play, I struggled badly. I could hardly run, and I knew it was never going to work.

John Coughlin also never made the start to the season he had hoped and he decided to step down. He was replaced by his player–coach Gus MacPherson. I knew that was the time to call it quits. It was then I spoke to Gus and told him there was no point in me still being at St Mirren. I said that if he could get a package for me then I would go because I was struggling, and it might also give him the chance to bring in some of his own players. I went and spoke to the chairman Stewart Gilmour, and we quickly thrashed out a severance package.

A lot of people will be reading this and thinking I had a cheek to ask for anything, and they would be right. St Mirren gave me a substantial cheque to leave, although I kidded myself on by saying that I would have actually saved them money in tax if I had just stayed and ran down my contract. If I am being honest, getting my deal terminated was a godsend. It was a blessing in disguise. My football days were over. I wanted out. I was completely scunnered with the game, and it was time to make a new start doing something totally different with my life.

My time at St Mirren isn't exactly a period in my life I can look back on with great pride. I let so many people connected with the club down, none more so that John Coughlin. He had shown great faith in me and I had given him next to nothing in return. I got a decent wage by St Mirren's standards, and I also got money to leave. I never went to any other club in my career solely for money, although at times it was a major factor. I was coming to the end of my career and I just went to St Mirren for one final payday. I had my injury problems and I wasn't fit enough to play. I had been through hell with my neck at Hearts. There was next to no chance of St Mirren ever seeing the best of me on a football pitch come a Saturday afternoon. It was strange because every other club I had been at I really enjoyed and wanted to be there, but at St Mirren I didn't and there was only one person to blame, and that was myself. I was also coming through from Edinburgh and the travelling killed me. I just couldn't be bothered with it. I didn't want to be at St Mirren, I didn't want to play football. If any St Mirren fan is reading this now, then I can only say that I'm sorry. If I could turn back the clock I would, but the damage has been done, I know. It was a dark period in my life and was probably even darker for the fans who had to watch me in action when I pulled on that black and white shirt that means so much to so many people.

I had to decide what I wanted to do after St Mirren, and this time I knew professional football was no longer an option. It was a chance to start afresh and I had to work out what I wanted to do. I decided I wanted to go into football coaching. I was lucky enough to get the chance to start working with Midlothian Council coaching local kids, while I also gave it another season playing for the junior side Penicuik Thistle. I worked at Midlothian Council under Neil Orr, the former West Ham United and Hibs defender. The council put me through my Scottish Football Association early touches badges, and that enabled me to take the first step on the coaching ladder. I enjoyed it, but it wasn't full time and didn't bring regular hours. Some weeks it might be fifteen hours and the next it might be ten. It was basically a part-time job, and I wasn't making enough money. I wasn't getting enough to bet and so I continued to look elsewhere to get money. I was also doing a few jobs here and there, including painting, but I was primarily coaching.

I stopped the coaching in 2005 and I started working in the Close Circuit Television with Lothian and Borders Police. I got that job because one of the two main bosses there was a big Rangers fan. He knew I was big friends with my ex-Motherwell teammate and the Ibrox legend Andy Goram, and that was a big factor in me getting the job. He loved his football and all the gossip of the game. My friend, Stevie Curran, was also working there, so I basically walked into that job.

I have to say that even though I was handed a half-decent position, my attitude was still absolutely terrible. My effort and commitment were non-existent. It was probably one of the best jobs I could have asked for, but I treated it like it was a load of rubbish and below me. This was a job that should have been done properly, but I gave it nowhere near the 100 percent commitment it deserved. It was an important job, I was meant to be there to see nothing was kicking off and to make sure the general public were safe, but that was probably at the bottom of my priorities. I actually saw a few things that were absolutely horrific in my time in that job, including a young boy being murdered. That really traumatised me. I couldn't sleep for days after that, my bosses even asked me if I needed help or support. I didn't really think it had affected me, but it did. It was horrible seeing a young teenager die. I was warned and it was part of my initial training that I might witness some horrible things, that was why the team had its own specialised trauma team. I also saw some distressing attacks on people as well. The streets of Scotland's capital can be a tough place.

I was also no longer on the big sort of wages I had been used to when I was a footballer. My money wasn't going far, especially when it came to my gambling. I was also being forced to pay back bits and bobs, although I had very little choice in the matter. My finances – or lack of them – was a major issue. A company had taken over all my debts and my wages. They were basically taking my wages and using them to pay off all my debts over a longer period of time. It allowed me to try and get myself sorted out but it also came at a cost, as the interest rates the company charged were astronomical. That was the official debts I had, but there were still unofficial debts which led to some mad and undesirable people chasing after me.

I had numerous people coming to my parents' door looking for money, from sheriff officers to really unscrupulous characters. The phone was going twenty-four/seven, with people looking to threaten me. My mum and dad didn't know half the stuff that was going on because most nights I would put their phone on silent to stop it ringing. The last thing I wanted to do was have them answering the phone and knowing what I had got myself embroiled in.

I also started laying bets, where I would act as the bookmaker and give people odds on a horse or a football match. It was pretty much glorified stealing. I might give people 4–1 or 5–1 on a bet. Even if they won they had no chance of getting their winnings because I didn't have it. I knew that when I was taking the bets, but I was just hoping their punts wouldn't come up and I could walk away with the money and gamble it away myself. I have been lucky because even the bets I did take I managed to talk my way out of, and because I could quite easily have taken a good few batterings, but most of the time I came through relatively unscathed.

It will come as no surprise that I lost my job in the CCTV unit at the start of 2005. I got caught going away early from work one night. My boss had let me go but then his superior found out. They looked back the videotapes and they clearly showed me going away early. I held my hands up. There was no point in lying. They told me that if I wanted to walk away with a clean slate, then I could go now, and it would give me another chance of getting another job with the council. They also said that if I took them to a tribunal I wouldn't have a leg to stand on, because they could check the monitors and they showed that the cameras hadn't been moved, which they were supposed to do all the time when I was working. They also warned me that they might also need to get the police involved if I went down that route. I was basically left with no option but to walk out the door.

To be fair, my head was in a complete mess. That was when I was at my lowest. I would have done anything for money. I look back and I feel my boss should also have been sacked as well, but I was the only one who took the wrap. It was so stupid, people were always leaving the office early, but I ended up becoming the fall guy for them all. I should never have agreed to go, but mentally I was just so screwed up. Gambling had me where it wanted me, and it was never going to let go.

I left there and then, and I started to sign on. That was in the February to March of 2005. I had gone from hero to zero in the space of a couple of years. My relationship was also on the rocks, and I was heading towards September and that taxi ride which would end up with me finally hitting rock bottom.

18

PLAYING AND BLOWING
MY FAMILY FORTUNES

Over the years, I have also stolen a lot of money from my parents, and my mum in particular. I never went to my dad for cash because he would have known I wanted it to bet. I always went and asked my mum because she was a softer touch and was less likely to say no. By then, my greed for gambling had no boundaries. Not content with just asking for cash from my mum, I then started to steal from her as well. I would take her bank cards and go and empty a lot of money out of her account. I am not talking about £20 or £50 here or there. I stole tens of thousands of pounds from my mum.

At first she didn't really notice because I was taking small amounts that I could sneak out without her realising. When you have a gambling problem, no matter how much money you have, it is never enough. It wouldn't matter if you were on the dole or the richest man on the planet, because when betting takes over your life, you are willing to wager everything you have or you can get your hands on. Gambling can push you to extremes, to a place where you are completely out of control. A compulsive gambler who steals is unlikely to steal large sums of money, especially initially, because they know there is more chance of them getting caught. My mum had a wee bit of money, cash she had worked hard to get and save, but I thought nothing about taking it off her and putting it on a horse, dog or a football team. It was a case of easy-come, easy-go.

My withdrawals from my mum's account became more and more frequent, and the withdrawals were getting bigger and bigger. My mum starting to notice what I was draining out of her account because I was suddenly taking hundreds of pounds out at a time. My mum challenged me and asked me what I was doing, but I had the gift of the gab and I was always able to lie myself out of trouble. What I did to my parents, you just wouldn't believe. I caused so much animosity and pain between my mum and dad. I probably drove a real wedge between them because of my own selfish ways and my gambling. I am sure there were times when they came close to splitting up and ending their marriage because of my selfish antics. My mum, nine times out of ten, would stick up for me, while my dad would be more likely to challenge me or have a go at me. That would cause real friction between them. I could see it happening, but I was more than happy with the situation knowing that I could use it to my advantage, as my mum would continually stand by me. I didn't really bat an eyelid at what impact my gambling had on my mum, my dad, their life or their marriage.

The ironic thing is that my mum would never take any nonsense from anybody in any other walk of life. You could probably describe my mum as formidable, but when it came to me I was her Achilles heel. Most people in Danderhall know her because she used to be the bar manager at the local club. She would never stand for any trouble or rubbish, and she was never slow in telling people what she thought. She has also worked in shops and at Pollock Halls, which is a big campus for university students in Edinburgh. She worked really hard to make sure my sister Nicola and I never wanted for anything, even if it meant her working two jobs or all the hours God sent. She would always give us money, and if she didn't have it, then my nana would be there to lend a hand.

I tore my mum to pieces with my gambling and what I did to her. I had my mum over a barrel. She would never tell my dad what I had done because I would blackmail her emotionally. I would say things like, 'If you tell Dad I will never speak to you again.' I was out of control. To be fair to my mum, she didn't tell my dad until near the end, when I was at the height of my troubles and when things were really bad. Money was going missing from her bank account left, right and centre, and at that point it was obvious to everybody that I needed help.

I was always trying to cover my tracks. I would wait for the post, and as soon as anything official came in I would hide it, rip it up or put it in the bucket. There were also the phone calls or the chaps at the door. One evening my dad answered the phone from a credit company, and at that point he asked me what was going on. My dad was furious when he came off the phone. He got really annoyed with me, and quite rightly so, because his house was down as my address to a debt-collecting company, even though it should have had absolutely nothing to do with him or my mum.

Dad and I started to have more and more arguments, and I didn't help the situation because I wasn't being open and honest about the mess I was in. I was never really that close to my dad, but that was because he knew what I was like and he could see right through me. I was always a mummy's boy because I knew I could wrap my mum round my finger, and I could never do that with my dad. I could never do anything wrong in my mum's eyes, and there is no doubt I played on that.

The way I frittered away such a lot of money must have been so hard for them because I know they have both worked so hard to get everything they have. I have also taken so much money off them, they have got that all back now, but that is only part of the debt I know I owe them.

My mum and dad certainly didn't deserve to be treated the way I treated them. They are both genuinely great people. I couldn't have asked for better parents. They are both as honest as the day is long. They have both done so much for Nicola and I. They shouldn't have been put in the awful situation I put them in.

I am just so proud and more than a bit relieved that, throughout everything, they have remained strong and together, although it was no thanks to me. I am so pleased they are still together because I know how close I came to splitting them up. It also shows in a positive way just how strong my mum and dad's relationship really is. If they could survive me at my worst, then their marriage could survive anything because I know I caused them both so much heartache. The damage I did and saw was bad enough, I hate to think of all the other issues and problems I didn't see when I was out the house.

My dad was a miner and worked at Monktonhall. When I was younger he used to put a lot of extra shifts in to get some additional money for the family. One of the earliest memories of my dad was during the time when there was the massive miners' strike of the mid-1980s, when Arthur Scargill tried to take on the prime minister at that time, Margaret Thatcher. My dad went out on strike and I remember we had some tough times as a family during that period. My dad was a staunch miner and refused to cross a picket line. The majority of my dad's friends and comrades were all of a similar ilk and would never have considered crossing a picket line or going back down the mines. There were one or two others, who were nicknamed 'scabs', who decided to break rank, but they were few and far between.

There were times where money was tight and we probably were on the breadline, but I still never really wanted for anything. Anything I wanted or asked for, within reason, I knew my mum would get me. When my dad was out on strike it was left to my mum to try and make ends meet, and that also led to some trying times in the house. My mum wanted my dad to go back to work for the sake of us, but he was determined to stick to his principles and was never ever going to go back. We also received food parcels and handouts from the miners' unions, although it wasn't a lot, but every little helped. My mum was also quite a proud person and she wasn't looking for charity, she just wanted my dad back out working and helping to support the family.

It is quite funny because we still have a newspaper cutting of my dad from the time of the strike. He went down to Yorkshire on a mini-bus from Danderhall to support their strike down there. He ended up getting arrested. There is a photograph of him in a newspaper getting carried out by eight policemen and the caption said: This Man was Carried Away Shouting, 'This Is a Police State'. That shows how passionate he was about mining and what was being done to an industry he loved. The strike went on for months, and nearer the end I thought there would come a day when my dad would go back to coal mining, but he never did.

That was probably the stage of my early life where I saw my dad the most. He never really had a part to play when I was growing up because I was never that close to him. I was always a mummy's boy, even though my dad watched quite a lot of my football as I was growing up. I played for Danderhall Primary School, where the best memory for me there was when we beat Mayfield 3–2 at Bonnyrigg in a Cup final, and I managed to grab a hat-trick. I was in Primary 6, while most of the others were a year older. A lot of the boys who played in that game are still my friends today, like my cousin Kenny Wilson, Andy Davidson, Davie Peacock and Jamie Murray.

My dad also travelled all over Scotland to watch me play professional football. I know my dad would always tell people he was so proud of me, but he would never say it to my face. That was because I had put him and my mum through so much with my stealing, lying and gambling. My dad knew some of the things I had done to my mum and other people, and I know the wedge that was there was down to me and my gambling. He has seen first-hand some of the carnage that I have caused.

Yet in my hour of need, my dad was there for me. If it hadn't been for him, I would have gone to jail for fraud because I had stolen to get more money to gamble. At that point, I had completely lost it and I would have done anything for money, and I mean anything. That was how deep I was in. If my dad hadn't bailed me out and given me the money to clear my debts, then I would have ended up behind bars, there is no doubt about that. I probably didn't deserve the support and financial backing he gave me. It shows just what kind of person he is, even after everything I had done to him and my mum.

My dad stumped up a massive five-figure sum to save me from having to go to prison. I know it was money he didn't have, but he still went and took out a loan to get me what I needed. I owed a lot of money, a hell of a lot of money, to people and companies who I had been stupid enough to take from. That was at the same time I was coaching kids at the Council and working for the police in the CCTV unit in Edinburgh, but just through fraudulent things I had done, involving individuals and big companies, I had put myself in real trouble and in real danger.

But my mum and dad aren't the only members of my family that I have stolen from. The lengths I have gone to gamble would make people cringe with embarrassment and probably leave others feeling extremely angry that somebody could do what I have done to my own flesh and blood. I have robbed from my dying nana and my Auntie Margaret, and I was also in the wildest throes of gambling when my niece Kelsa was born. I went up to the hospital with my mum and dad, but I really didn't want to be there, even though I am probably one of the most protective uncles in the whole world. I didn't want to be anywhere but in a bookies' or in front of a television watching races and dogs or horses that I had punted heavily on.

Kelsa's birth actually gave my life a bit of a temporary shake-up. I was still gambling, but Nicola had split up with Kelsa's dad, and I had decided it was up to me to be like a second father to the wee one, so I could be there for her and protect her. When my sister told me Kelsa had been born, I ended up in floods of tears. I was really emotional and I had never really been like that in my life before. Not that the new me, the father figure, lasted long. I was soon back to my bad old ways and stooping to new lows. I even started to steal money from Kelsa's piggy bank. I also took money out of her bank account and just blew it on betting, even though she was only a wee baby. By the time she was three or four, I had spent most of the savings she had. I can't remember how much it was exactly, but it was more than a thousand pounds. I just can't believe I could do that to my wee niece.

What I have done to people who are closest to me hurts and embarrasses me the most. Some of the things I have done are still hard to stomach. I have to live with these things every day. What it has done has made me even more determined to sort myself out and to try and make people proud of me again. And

I especially owe my parents so much. They would probably disagree, but I am so riddled with guilt and remorse that I genuinely believe that. They have done nothing but support me, but I know I have let them down. They have been the perfect parents, but I know I have been far from the perfect son.

19

FATHERLY AND FRIENDLY FAILINGS

Emma was born on 1 August 1989. It should have been one of the happiest days of my life, but I didn't even want to be at the birth. In fact, I chose not to be there when Emma was born. I left my former girlfriend, Jill, who was two and a half months pregnant when we started going out, to go through the whole process with her family and mine. I was nowhere to be seen. I had decided I didn't want to be there. Don't ask me why, because even now I struggle to explain my reasons for that crazy decision. I can't even remember where I was. I was probably in the bookies or betting on something. That was at the time when I was still working as a painter, and it wasn't as if I was making millions, but now with hindsight, I can see I had my priorities all wrong.

If I am being truthful, I probably wasn't ready to become a dad. I was only seventeen. I could hardly keep my life or my betting in order, so how was I ever going to be able to become a father to a child? I suddenly had responsibilities in my life and that was something that scared me more than anything. Before that my main task was checking that day's form and getting my bets on before that first football match or dog or horse race got under way. Emma's arrival should have been something of a culture shock to my life, but did it really change things that much? I would question whether or not it did because I still continued with my carefree ways and left Jill, more often than not, to get on with things.

It was definitely immaturity on my part that I wasn't at Emma's birth. I know now I should have been there for Emma and to support Jill. Don't get me wrong. I was still absolutely delighted when Emma was born, and I still remember the joy when I saw her little face for the first time. It was an amazing feeling, but I also have to admit there was a fair bit of trepidation in the bargain, wondering how I was going to cope with the responsibility, both physically and financially, of parenthood.

The funny thing now is that children and family are now at the centre of my world. If my wife Jac and I were lucky to have a child, then there is no doubt I would be there for every single second of the birth. I genuinely can't think of anywhere else I would rather be, but first time around I tried to avoid parenthood at all costs.

The ironic thing is that when Emma's son Jack was born, I went straight up to the hospital. Nothing could have kept me away. I was there when Emma was in the middle of her labour, and I was back to see her and the wee one first thing the next morning. They are a massive part of my life, although I know Emma should have already played a far greater part in my life. I love seeing Emma and Jack, and I have a great bond with the wee one. It just goes to show, all these years on, I could take Emma's hand and assure her I was there for her when she was in labour, but back in the days of my gambling, I would never have dreamt of doing anything like that for her or Jill.

Was I there as much as I should have been for Emma? Definitely not. I was never really there for her. I was there sporadically, but not all the time when she needed me. Jill and I, not surprisingly, had our ups and downs at times, and there were periods when Emma saw a lot less of me than she should have. I know now what your own child should mean to you, and I know when Emma was born I definitely didn't appreciate her enough. I don't know if I was just young or stupid or if that was down to the gambling, because I now know what being a dad is all about.

I never had a great relationship with Emma when she was growing up, and that is something I am ashamed to admit. There were times when I would give her everything, but there were other times when I never gave her as much time as I should have. So when I did give her things, I probably over-compensated because I felt I had let her down in other aspects of her life. I know I should have given her more time and attention. Any child needs the care and love of their parents, but Emma never got that from me. I would never have seen anything happen to Emma, but at times I know she found it hard. She said to me there were periods when I wasn't really like a dad to her, and she is probably right. How can I argue? It was hard to hear her say that, but it was even harder to take because I knew how true it was. It was down to gambling, and I know I had my priorities all wrong.

It was a continuing trend of my life. Even when I was making big money at Motherwell I still hardly gave Jill a penny to support Emma. I wouldn't even have got a mortgage with the mess I was in financially. That is some admission from someone who had been earning good money in football for six or seven years.

When I was at Motherwell, my gambling wasn't just taking my money, but it was also taking a lot of what should have been family time. I would think nothing of leaving poor Emma sitting outside on the doorstep for hours after school because I was in the bookies. There were other times where she would have to sit in a car for hours waiting for me to finish betting. She wasn't looking for anything physical like money, all she wanted was some time and affection from me, and I hardly gave her either. I only had time for betting.

You have to remember that betting and your behaviour can also have an effect on children, but when you are betting you don't really consider anyone else when you are in the midst of a gambling frenzy. Children whose parents or guardians or siblings have betting problems can feel forgotten. I can understand and vouch for that in the way I treated Emma at times. I've heard about cases where children feel they are the cause of the betting problem because their parents don't want to spend time with them. I wouldn't say that was the case with Emma and me, but gambling certainly became an addiction, and it definitely caused me to lose focus on life and the people I really cared about.

I also treated Jill really shabbily at times throughout the years. I remember when we first moved into our flat in Dalkeith. I was playing for Raith Rovers, and I was an absolute nightmare. The only time Jill got money off me was when I was on a winning run with my gambling, which, believe me, wasn't that often. It was Jill who kept a roof over our heads by going out and working two jobs. I had a real chance to give Jill and Emma something back, but I chose not to take it. I do feel embarrassed and ashamed at how I treated them. The one positive for me is that they stuck by me and still remain a massive part of my life, even though I treated them abysmally. I never gave them the time I should have. I hardly paid for anything. I look back on my life now and Emma and Jill have probably been the two biggest losers when it comes to me, because of everything I have done to them. They were involved in every bit of carnage I caused, even though at times I didn't really know what I was doing. I was under the total control of gambling.

I have taken so much money off Jill. It would have been well into five figures that I stole off her just so I could bet. I was content enough to blow my own wages, but that wasn't enough. I wanted more, even though Jill seemed to be working more hours than God.

When I was at Raith Rovers, I had gone on holiday to Ibiza with my teammate and friend Craig Dargo. We were only back a couple of days when I decided I was going to go away to Malaga. Jill didn't even know I was going. I just went. I didn't even phone her and tell her where I was until I was in Spain. I was a complete user and a horrible person. I certainly wasn't born like that. I wasn't always like that, but it was down to the gambling. Even when I was away I was phoning home to put my bets on. By that time I was gambling heavily and that was my sole focus. It definitely changed me as a person.

I remember going to the casino in Glasgow one night with my former Motherwell teammate Roberto Martinez, who has since gone on to manage Swansea and Wigan Athletic. He was staying in the Moorings Hotel in Motherwell on his own, and so he spent a bit of time at our house. We used to like going out for a meal and then to the casino. Roberto liked a bet, but he knew when to call it quits. That is why he has earned good money and invested wisely, while I went the opposite way. On this visit to the casino with Roberto, I won £38,000 playing cards at the tables. I took it home in £50 and £100 notes, and then stuck it in a carrier bag under the bed. All the money was in bundles in this plastic bag.

I got up the next morning before heading for training, took £3,000 out of the bag and took it downstairs to where Jill was getting Emma ready for school. I told her that I had won £3,000 at the casino. She wasn't really that bothered. She knew what I was like and said to me, 'Yes. Great. You have won £3,000, but how much have you lost to actually win it?' She knew the score and was certainly a lot more switched on than me. I told her we could split the £3,000. I'd give Emma and her both £1,000 and leave £1,000 for me. She didn't seem too impressed, but eventually she agreed.

After training I went shopping and bought myself £1,000 worth of Armani gear. That night I went back to the casino. I took all the money I had won the previous night with me. I didn't leave a penny of it in the house. I knew I was going to blow it all, and I did precisely that. I lost all of the £35,000 left from my winnings and another £600 on top of that. I actually thought I was still a winner because I had bought £1,000 worth of clothes, so I hadn't gambled every single penny away, that was how sick I was. Looking back, it just goes to show what a state I was in. I didn't see anything wrong with losing the money. I didn't go to the casino to lose it, but I didn't want to win either because I still had the thrill of winning the previous night.

Jill and I weren't getting on too well come the end of my time at Motherwell. She spent a lot of her time back in Edinburgh, while I remained in Motherwell. We had pretty much come to an end and she knew my gambling was out of hand. I also was terrible to her. I wasn't the person I should have been. I treated her really poorly. I said I had had enough, but I also knew she had had enough of me. Who could blame her? We agreed that would be it. Our relationship was over before Motherwell had even gone into administration. Emma stayed with me because she was still at school. It was probably the best thing Jill could have done for herself and for Emma.

Gambling has also killed relationships with other former partners outwith Jill. I gave them next to no time at all. I remember another occasion when I went up to Aberdeen for my birthday with a long-term girlfriend. We were staying at the Thistle Hotel in Cove, on the outskirts of the Granite City. My girlfriend made a real effort. She went and prepped the room and dressed it with balloons and banners. But, according to me at the time, she completely wasted her time. I went to the bar for a so-called quick drink. I went downstairs and the Motherwell team, who were due to play Aberdeen, were also staying in the hotel. I proceeded to spend the next couple of hours talking to some of my old teammates and playing the bandit. I might have been in conversation with some of the players, but I was only really there so I could play the slot machine. It wasn't as if I was sitting there drinking the house dry. I have never been a big drinker. I just wanted to gamble, even if it was only 30p a spin. When I finally decided to drag myself back up to the room, my girlfriend was already in her bed. She was breaking her heart crying. Looking back now, I was a complete idiot. I treated her so badly and that is something I feel awful about. I think after that night she knew the writing was on the wall for our relationship.

I started to spend less and less time with her. I was also telling her lies all the time. She would phone and ask me where I was. Nine times out of ten, when I could be bothered to take her call, I was in the bookies. I never ever told her where I was. I treated her like rubbish and did some horrible things to her. We'd had holidays booked and I forced her to cancel them at the last minute. There was one occasion, in March 2005, when I booked and paid for a holiday, but then I went on a mad betting frenzy days before we were due to go away. I didn't have a penny left to my name. I had wagered everything, including our spending money for the holiday. I was meant to be taking her away, but in the end I couldn't go because I didn't have a bean left. I didn't even tell her the truth. I made up some lame excuse and tried to cover my tracks, like most gambling addicts do. I made up some story that I had lost my passport and I couldn't go, so we both ended up missing out on a holiday that I had bought and paid for.

I didn't give my behaviour a second thought. I didn't really think how I was treating her or what I was doing to her. Our relationship was probably never the same again after that. It was hardly a surprise, if I am being honest. She should have got up and left me there and then. That incident was the start of a real downward spiral between us. I think with all the lies I was telling and the way I had treated her she had finally started to open her eyes to everything and the more sinister side of me.

I do have a lot of guilt over the way I treated her. Christmases and birthdays are meant to be special times, but it all depended how my betting form had gone around those particular times. It really came down to how much money I had left to spend, if any. I probably paid for very little when we were together. In fact, I think I paid for next to nothing.

She was always at me for us to get a flat together. She kept asking when we would move in together. I just palmed her off with excuse after excuse. She was staying with her mum and I was still at home with my mum and dad back in Danderhall. It was my fault because I had led her up the garden path and made her a lot of false promises.

When I first met her she was going away to work on a cruise ship in St Mark's in the Caribbean. I only met her a couple of months before she was due to go away. I remember she had a big leaving party and I asked her not to go. I thought she was the girl I was going to marry, and I told her that. I pleaded with her not to go. She told me that she needed to go because she had always wanted to go and work on the cruise ships. She had done beauty treatments since about the age of sixteen til she was twenty-three, and this was something she had set her heart on doing. She did go away, but we still remained in contact. Within a few days, she told me that she wanted to come back because she was really missing me, but she wanted to know that I was serious and I wanted to settle down with her. I told her I did, and convinced her to come back. When she returned to Edinburgh, it was more a boyfriend–girlfriend thing than anything more serious. If I am being honest, I was once again scared of the commitment. I didn't want anything to do with laying down roots. The only thing I was really interested in was gambling. As long as I had enough money for a bet, then I was fine. I wasn't interested in buying a flat or a house where I would need to spend money on everyday things and bills. I wanted all my money for gambling. She ended up buying a flat and moving in with one of her friends because she was sick of waiting for me to leave my parents.

I also played a lot of pool and I got my girlfriend to get money off her uncle to sponsor me. He owned his own painting firm. He gave me £800 and that was to help get me through that year's tour. I also got another businessman from Dalkeith to give me £1,000. That money was to cover my expenses for the pool season, but I gambled every single penny, although I didn't tell anyone that I had blown the money. I was lucky because I was able to cover up. I managed to borrow and scrape enough money to fulfil my pool commitments, although I should never have put myself in that position. I feel really terrible because I know for a fact that my former partner had gone out of her way to help me and to get her uncle to sponsor me. I wasn't interested. I didn't even give her a second thought. I was just thinking of ways how I could deceive or squeeze even more money out of people.

I must have borrowed thousands of pounds off of her. I did pay it all back, but it was a long time after we had finished and I was back on the straight and narrow. By the time we eventually split up, I owed her a lot of money. I can now say that I have given her all that money back, although I still owe her an awful lot more that money would never cover.

Don't get me wrong. We had a lot of happy times together, but I didn't treat her the way I should have. I couldn't even tell her I had a gambling problem, so what chance did we have? It all came to an end because I wouldn't move on and commit. So she did what she should have done a long time earlier and walked away from me to get on with her own life.

I know I still have a lot to thank her for because if it hadn't been for her words in the taxi that night, I would not be in the position I am in today. If she hadn't woken me up, then who knows what I might've become. I might have dropped even further into that dark pit of despair and misery, and who knows where it would have led me? Maybe to even more stealing, heavier fraud or even suicide. Thankfully now I will never know because she helped me find my rock bottom and the point where I was able to turn my life around.

She has moved on with her life and I have moved on with mine. I wish things had turned out differently and that I hadn't been such an idiot. It was my own fault. I still miss her family because they are lovely people and didn't deserve all the rubbish I selfishly put their daughter and them through.

I gave all my girlfriends very little time at all. I look back at what these people and their families gave me and I gave them absolutely nothing in return. Maybe a small percentage of the real me, if they were lucky. That is the thing about compulsive gambling. It takes away everything and doesn't care as long as you are able to put that next bet on. You think when you are gambling that you are only hurting yourself, but only when you manage to break that cycle, you realise the damage you have done to other people round you.

And I had done a huge amount of damage to so many people. I had borrowed money, stolen it from my dying nana, from my niece, not paid back my debts to family and friends, done anything and everything I could to get my hands on cash, no matter who I hurt. My addiction changed me from the person that people knew into this other person, basically a lowlife who had no interest in anything other than gambling and getting the buzz that reckless gambling gave me time and time again, no matter what the cost.

I had been living my life like this for years, slowly but surely getting out of control, realising what was happening at times but always ignoring the nagging voice inside me that knew I shouldn't be gambling like I was. Until I was out of control. Earning great money and gambling the lot, never caring if I won a bet but only if I had enough money to bet again. It's a down-ward spiral of addiction and destruction that just gets faster and faster until you reach a point of no return, a dark place where you no longer have any control over your life, owing fortunes that you can never hope to pay back and losing so much more than money – your friends, your family and yourself.

For me, this had been a long time coming. Years, in fact. And then I had got to the point where I bought the pills and decided I would end my life – until I realised that I couldn't go through with it. I thought that was rock bottom for me, as low as things could get, but I was still months away from that point, when it all hit me and it was time to finally face up to the real me, what I had become and to my addiction.

On the night of the taxi journey with my then girlfriend that was to change my life, I had absolutely no idea that the world I had built around me was about to completely collapse. For me, it was just another night out, having some fun and a few drinks. And then, there I was in that taxi with my girlfriend, finally being told what a huge disappointment I was, how I had done so much and yet had absolutely nothing to show for my life, told to go away and sort myself out because I was basically a disgrace. That my life was a sham. That because of my gambling, I was nothing.

I suppose it was the first time that somebody had really understood the extent of my problem and had confronted me in such a brutally honest way. And for whatever reason, it hit home like a sledgehammer. With everything else that was going on in my life and all the things in my head, it was the last straw for me. It just triggered a moment when I could see the horrible truth of what she was saying to me which allowed me to acknowledge the part of me that, deep down, knew my life was a sham and had to drastically change now – otherwise there might be no more chances.

That moment was like a revelation for me. I could have ignored it and carried on with my life the way it was, but somehow I knew I had reached rock bottom and knew I had to finally find a way to face up to reality. But taking the first step on that journey was never going to be easy.

20

THE FIRST STEP
ON THE ROAD TO RECOVERY

That first morning after I had hit rock bottom was a strange day. I had to tell the world I had a gambling problem. My dad, ironically, got up early because he was going to York for the horse racing, believe it or not. I didn't say anything to him. I decided to stay in my bed and wait until he had left. I didn't feel it was right to burden him before his trip. I just lay on my bed for a bit, but I knew I had to make a start and tell somebody.

I am really close to my sister Nicola, and I decided that she should be the first person I should tell. I went to her house, chapped her door and opened my heart to her. Nicola has always been somebody I have been able to confide in. I still remember the moment, as clear as day, when I broke down and told her I had a gambling problem. I completely lost it. I was in tears and shaking. I was a physical and mental wreck. I wasn't the same brother that she knew, loved and had grown up with.

Nicola knew I liked to have a wee bet, but she had no idea how bad my addiction was. Nobody did. She also burst into tears as I told her how my life had gone into self-destruct mode. I then went on to tell Nicola of some of the despicable things I had done, like stealing money out of Kelsa's bank account so I could bet. I kept telling her I needed to get help. Nicola, to be fair, was really supportive. She was like a rock for me that day. I couldn't have blamed her if she had thrown me out after some of my shocking confessions. I mean, I had stolen off my own little niece, her daughter, a lovely wee kid. If she had thrown me out, though, I don't know where I would have ended up. I kept telling her I needed help. Nicola was just so strong. She said she was proud of me for owning up to my problems and that Kelsa and she would be there for me. They would be there to help me and keep me on the road to recovery.

Knowing they were behind me was a big thing for me. It gave me the inner strength and confidence that maybe, with a wee bit of help, I could turn things around. We both agreed that my next port of call should be to tell my mum and dad.

I left Nicola's house at nine in the morning. From there I decided there was one more visit I had to make before I returned home to my parents. I was aware of another professional footballer who had similar problems. I knew him well, and I went and chapped his door. He had played professional football at the highest level and I knew he was attending Gamblers Anonymous. I knew he would be able to help me and give me a bit of guidance on how I could get help. I spoke to the player and his mum. It was all still very raw to me and, once again, I broke down in tears and confessed all to them.

Right away the player said he knew what I was going through. He had been down the exact same path. He told me there was a Gamblers Anonymous meeting in Edinburgh on the Monday evening and he would take me. That was a massive help. His words lifted a huge weight off my shoulders. I have to admit, I was worried and apprehensive about the prospect of walking into a room full of strangers and then unburdening all my problems and issues on him. Having somebody there for a bit of moral support at least gave me a bit of reassurance. I wanted to go to the GA meeting to see if it would help me. I knew it was time to stop betting – to quit gambling my life away.

The next big thing was to tell my mum. I would have to wait to tell my dad until he came back on the Sunday night. My mum was aware of my gambling. She was absolutely devastated when I told her. She was crushed that her son had made such a mess of his life. I am sure she also felt guilty that she hadn't seen how bad my problems were, but my parents had nothing to feel guilty about. Everything was my own doing. I was the only one to blame. It was then I probably witnessed for the first time the damage I had not only done to myself, but also the people round me, those closest to me. That realisation was harder for me than actually telling my mum. Like Nicola, she promised to do whatever she could and to try and get me out of the hole I was in.

I went through that weekend and I never had a single bet. That was the first time I had gone that length of time without a punt for more than twenty-five years. I still had a couple of quid in my pocket, not a lot, but enough to put money on a horse or a coupon. But I didn't. And possibly for the first time I thought, 'Maybe I can go a length of time without gambling.'

The Sunday evening my dad came home was the first time I really sat down and spoke to him. I never had confided in him much, since I had always been closer to my mum. He also was aware of my gambling and probably of how much damage I had done to myself, although he maybe didn't know how deep it had put me in debt. He was aware of a lot of things that I had done wrong. My dad had said to me hundreds of times things like, 'You've been standing at that bandit (a slot machine) for hours,' or, 'You are never out of the bookies.' He had said things like that but had never confronted me and said, 'Kevin, you have a problem.' I am not blaming my dad because it was my issue and my doing. I just wonder if somebody close to me had challenged me about my gambling earlier then maybe I would have confronted things a lot earlier than I did. Then again, it might have made absolutely no difference.

Looking back to that night, it was absolutely demoralising because I had never ever seen my dad as upset as he was then. I was in a flood of tears telling him the predicament I had got myself into. I still remember that evening. It broke his heart as well. It must have been an absolute nightmare for my parents to hear their son admit he had a serious gambling problem. It has be one of the worst scenarios that any parent can face. My dad, to be fair, was really supportive. He told me he was really proud of me of me facing up to the fact that I had a problem. I really admired the way my dad took it. I never expected him to act the way he did. My dad was very supportive and emotional, and that was a side of him I hadn't really seen. In saying that, it would almost be impossible to second-guess how any parent would react. He, like the rest of my immediate family, told me that he would be there for me for whatever I needed. He told me I had to go to Gamblers Anonymous, but by that point, I had already agreed to go.

My dad also told me he would back me in every way possible to help me kick my habit. I told him I was in a really bad way financially, that I was up to my neck in debt. The figures I owed were absolutely frightening, but he listened and then told me that my mum and he would help me, but first he wanted me to write down every penny I owed. He said they would help pay all the money back, but they wanted a promise I would go and seek help and make a real effort to turn my life around. I told him I would because in my heart of hearts that is what I wanted to do more than anything.

My mum and dad went over and above the call of duty. I really appreciated them sticking by me because they could have quite easily disowned me after everything I had done to them and put them through. They had given me a possible exit, one that wasn't there before. I was grateful and relieved, but I still couldn't help myself. I went to the local Danderhall club that Monday afternoon before the meeting. I think I only went there to test myself. I hadn't had a bet in three days and I felt in a good place mentally, probably as good as I had felt in years. There was an escape from my hell. My mum and dad were going to help bail me out. I was set to go to GA, and if I am being brutally honest, I hoped the meetings would stop me gambling, but I didn't think they would. My view was that there was nothing in the world that would stop me gambling, outwith maybe just ending it all.

I thought if I went to these meetings and my dad helped bail me out, then that would be great. I could sort myself out and then get back on the rollercoaster again. I had got out of it once and surely I could do it again. I should have felt like the luckiest man in the world that day, but I didn't. I still wanted to bet, despite everything I had said and promised to my family. I will tell you how stupid I was. That next day in the club I actually thought, 'Stuff it,' and I put a few bets on as I sat and watched the horse racing with a few of the boys. I ended up losing something like £25 to £30. It was a relatively small amount, but it didn't matter. It didn't matter if it was a penny or £1 million. The impact would have been exactly the same, especially if my mum and dad found out. They had gone out of their way to help me. I had already put them through hell. They were giving me a second chance to sort out my life, and I still couldn't stop gambling.

I remember my last bet. I put £15 on a horse to win. I was sitting there watching the television and I wasn't even wanting my horse to win. It didn't, and if I am being honest, I was probably quite happy about that. I know a lot of people who are reading this will think, 'Well, what is the point of gambling? Is it not the thrill of victory or that big-money win?' Well, to me, no, it wasn't. I wasn't gambling to win or make money. I was sick. It was an illness. I wanted to bet for the sake of doing it.

A lot of people who are in Gamblers Anonymous or have had problems with betting will tell you the same thing – they just betted to lose. To any sane person looking at things from the outside, that will seem like complete and utter madness. It is, but when gambling has got a hold of you, then you are only interested in feeding the addiction. I had lost the buzz for gambling. My fulfilment was putting the bet on and then seeing my money disappear. It didn't matter to me what I won because I knew it was never going to be enough. It would have just given me more to go away and blow. Come the end, I wanted to lose. I wanted people to see I had a problem. That way, I thought I could get the help I desperately needed. But up until that night in the taxi, I didn't think I was strong enough to address my problems on my own.

I started joking with the boys and some friends. That was me, now officially finished with gambling. I told them I wasn't going to bet again. They all knew me and were all rolling about laughing and joking. They knew how much I liked a punt and they thought there was no way in earth I would be able to walk away from it all. I also had the exact same view. They, however, didn't know what trouble I had got myself into, and that it was so bad I was having to go to GA that night.

21

ENTERING GAMBLERS ANONYMOUS

Monday, 3 October 2005 was the day I got my introduction to Gamblers Anonymous. I wanted to go to GA, but I genuinely didn't think it would stop me gambling. I didn't think there was anything or anyone who could stop me punting. I was a maniac when it came to betting. I was out of control.

It is funny because as soon as I left that first GA meeting, I knew I would never gamble again. It is hard to explain what caused the sudden change in my psyche. It was like somebody had flicked a switch in my head and it is impossible to explain how it happened. GA is just a weird, weird place, although in a good way. It was a life-changing experience for me. I still remember that first night. I was actually more worried that people would know me than I was to facing up to my gambling addiction, but when I walked into that first meeting that feeling went right out of the window. There were between twenty-five and thirty people, from all walks of life, sitting round in this horseshoe shape at that meeting. The professional footballer I had initially confided in and had come to the meeting with me, had also marked my card that there were a few other high-profile people and sportsmen who attended GA, and I would have nothing to worry about. I was in a real mess with betting, but I was still more worried about my ego than trying to seek help.

I remember we went round each person one by one and we all spoke about our problems. Some of the tales I heard were harrowing, even compared to everything I had been through. Eventually, my turn came. I remember sitting in my chair, all eyes on me. It became too much. I was very much a broken person and I just sat there in a mass of tears before I mustered enough strength and courage to stand and introduce myself. I had to give my first name and the initial of my surname, so I stood up, got a round of applause and said, 'I am Kevin T. and I am a compulsive gambler and I need help.'

It was hard saying that in front of so many people, but I quickly realised we were all in the same boat. We were all there for one reason – to try and get help. I told them some of the things I had done and the mess gambling had got me into. It was strange, after I had stood up and opened my soul I felt like a real weight had been lifted off my shoulders. After that, I just sat and listened to the experiences of other people and what gambling had done to them and their lives. I listened to every story and then I would think to myself, 'You do exactly the same things. Who are you to judge anyone else?' It really did help me open my eyes to the problem I had.

That meeting helped me get a handle on things. I remember I left that first meeting with a really strange feeling inside me. After listening to some of those people, I felt I could tell them everything. I had only known them for a couple of hours, but they were already like soul mates. I didn't want to let any of the people down, despite just meeting them for the first time. I had never met people like that before in my life. I felt that if I did gamble, I would not only be letting me and my family down, but them as well. That was something I wasn't prepared to do. I had done some awful things in my life, but letting them down really would have been the lowest of the low.

When you first go into GA, you are asked to answer twenty questions. The rule is that if you answer seven or more of these questions with a yes then it gives you an indication that you could be a compulsive gambler, but only you can decide whether or not you have a major issue. I felt it was quite intimidating when I tried to answer some of the questions because some of them are pretty full on. I managed to answer fourteen out of the twenty that first week. But when I went back again the next week, I managed to answer twenty out of twenty. I had probably tried to cover and be economical with the truth when I first answered the questions. If I am being honest, then I probably felt guilty about answering yes to some of the questions.

The final question of the twenty is: Have you ever considered suicide or taking your own life because of gambling? The answer was a simple: Yes. I had initially lied and said no the first week, but I knew if I was going to overcome the problem then I had to be honest and upfront with everyone, including myself. I was initially in denial. I had wanted to tell the truth that first night, but some of the questions I found hard to admit to.

Another question I struggled with was: Have you ever committed an illegal act to fund your gambling? I had also answered 'No' the first time. I was embarrassed to tell people that I had broken the law to help fund my betting. I quickly realised that if I wanted to turn the corner, then I had to be completely honest with myself and everybody else around me.

I now see people come through the doors at GA for the first time and I know, like me, they are very apprehensive about answering these questions honestly and openly in front of a room of total strangers. I now try and talk to people and tell them not to worry about the questions because we have all been in similar positions. They are not alone. They should try to be as honest as they can. I never had that sort of advice or guidance when I first walked into GA. I went in and answered those first fourteen questions maybe with blinkers on, and it was the wrong approach to take.

After I left that first meeting, I had two or three days without a bet, and the feeling was amazing. I never thought I could go that length of time without a bet. I had never gone that long without a punt before, even when I was abroad or away on holiday. I had always gambled. Even when I went on holiday with other people, they would be swimming in the sea or lying on the beach, and I would be sitting in a bookmakers somewhere or phoning home to get people to put bets on for me. So those first three days were incredible. I could live without a bet.

I couldn't put an exact figure as to what I had lost through gambling, though I would guess it was certainly into seven figures. What I lost more than anything was a lot of respect for myself. I have been very, very hard on myself. I have lived with so much remorse and guilt every day, sometimes even too much. People tell me I shouldn't keep burdening myself.

People who go to GA or who know me as a person will know what I mean. There are loads of sayings at GA, like 'You should look back but never stare.' I have lost so many friends and relationships, and that hurts me more than the money. Financially, I have lost more than a million pounds. I have never once looked back and said, 'Imagine if I had all that money now, what I could do with it.' The money is so immaterial to me. From the bottom of my heart, that is the honest truth. It is the things I have lost and done to people that cut me up every day.

Even when I spend time with my mum – she isn't keeping the greatest of health – I sometimes still go home and break my heart over what I have put her through. I may have caused her health to deteriorate and made her the anxious and worried person she can be at times. It might not be down to me, but I still blame myself and it kills me. That is how sore gambling has been to me. It took over my life and made me do so many wrongful things. People now say, 'Well, look at what you are doing to help people now and how big you are in GA.' I can look at myself in the mirror. I am no longer ashamed of what I see. I do try and do my best for myself, my family and everyone else, but it can still be hard at times. The main reason I now do what I do is to stop people having to go through what I have.

There are a lot of people I can say sorry to and there are a lot of people I could pay money back to, but there are other people who I have not seen to apologise to for what I have done. Whether some people would give me that chance, I don't know. There are people I have hurt and stolen from and they have every right not to accept my apology or to ever speak to me again. I know I have made a mug out of so many people, so many real friends. Even when I was at Hearts, there were some really good friends and people. Unfortunately, I don't see these people or maybe they just try to keep way from me because they no longer want anything to do with me. I know that I certainly couldn't blame them if they did.

I could have seen my mum and dad split up, I did things to my nana, watched her die and stole all her money, and there was also my Auntie Margaret who I also took money from before she passed away. These things just flash past in life, but at the time you don't give a damn about them or even a second thought about what you are doing to them because you are so engrossed in gambling.

If I could turn back the clock it would be for emotional reasons rather than financial ones. The damage has been as much mental as physical – as in stealing. I have put people through absolute hell through my own selfish actions. I think back now, and at times I get a bit of serenity.

If you are a compulsive gambler then you will always have an urge to bet. You never lose it, but you learn to control it. If somebody has been a compulsive gambler and tells you they no longer have an urge to bet, then I would go as far as calling them a liar. I could be totally wrong, but from my own experiences I just can't see somebody in that position ever losing that urge.

I try not to surround myself with people who gamble, but some of my best friends bet every day, but they are not compulsive gamblers. They are in control of what they are doing. They won't bet money they don't have. They only bet in moderation and wagers they can afford. I couldn't do that. When it came to gambling, it was all or nothing. I wasn't in for a penny, I was in for a pound. I also took a lot of people down with me as well. Nobody can say they would never get the urge to gamble again. I certainly couldn't. But I would never go back because I would hate to see somebody else end up in the same dark place where I had left myself.

If I ever did gamble again it would lead me back to my little bottle and a place I would never like to go back to ever again. I know if I bet even just once, I would be gambling with my life again. If I am being honest, I do miss betting so much, like nothing on earth. It is something I did every day and week in life for twenty-five years. But I know if I do go back to my bad old ways, I will have failed and let down so many people, including myself.

I still go back to my first Gamblers Anonymous meeting. Somebody said to me that when you want to gamble or think you want to have a bet, always go back to the lowest point, where betting left you completely broken. You put that real low point into words, write it on a bit of paper and then you have to put it in a little bottle that you carry with you every day. So if I ever feel like giving in and having a bet, then I get out my wee bottle and read my note. Inside that bottle is just a period of absolute despair and heartache. I was absolutely broken when I went to GA for the first time. People might laugh at the prospect of someone carrying a wee bottle around with them, but to me it is very significant as to what I have come through.

I am a very confident person and I tell people at GA that I will not gamble again, and I am certain I won't. I may get the urge, but I won't put on another bet as long as I live. If I do, then I can have no excuses and I would deserve everything I get. I know if I gamble again, my life would be over.

22

THE BUZZ OF GAMBLING

The pull and lure to gambling is the sheer rush of adrenalin that comes with it, that buzz and excitement of putting a bet on. That was a big thing for me. Also, when you are in a bookmakers or a casino, you feel like you are in your own little comfort zone. You have nobody bothering you, an escape from the outside world and no pressures from people chasing you for money. I honestly think I started gambling heavily because I couldn't cope with real life. That was my problem. I have started to realise that over the last couple of years. I just couldn't handle real life. I wasn't mature enough and couldn't accept the responsibilities of being an adult or a professional footballer. I had people chasing me for money that I didn't have. I just couldn't cope with those pressures. I was very immature and at times I tried to avoid reality.

In my experience, a lot of people who are compulsive gamblers are immature and struggle to cope with everyday pressures. If you speak to most people who gamble, especially those in foot-ball, they will tell you that they love to spend time in the bookies because it can offer a short-term escape from everything else.

I lost most of my money betting on horses, dogs, football and the casino. I never really bet online because that wasn't really big back then. I know it is massive now and is a big problem for a lot of men and women. I listen to people who come in to

Gamblers Anonymous say that they can gamble on anything online, from betting to the bingo and the lottery. I even used to play bingo with my mum just to gamble again.

I am not allowed to do anything which regards gambling now. I can't even put on a lottery ticket, football team fundraisers, scratch cards or even play bingo. I have to say, I am more than happy to sacrifice those things because I am now in total control of my life. When you first come in the door at GA, you are told you can do anything in life, one day at a time – apart from gamble. Certainly if you have a gambling problem, it must be an absolute nightmare whenever you switch on your television or computer. There seems to be twenty-four/seven advertising for online betting and gambling, especially if you are watching live sport.

The general perception of when you enter GA is you think you are going in amongst down-and-outs and people who have nothing. Near the end of my gambling, I was probably like that, but it could affect every person in society. I have seen brain surgeons, football players, cancer research workers, office workers, teachers and some of the most sophisticated and most intelligent people you could meet. You would never think by their jobs and where they are in their lives they would have such problems, but once again that shows you how secretive a disease gambling can be.

Another thing I have noticed is that there are more and more women who are coming to GA, which is incredible. Internet gambling seems to be the biggest vice for a lot of them. You can understand why, because more often than not, they probably feel quite intimidated walking into a bookies, since traditionally it is such a male-dominated place. Also by not going outside the house and mixing it allows them to keep their gambling under wraps. It really is harrowing, and I have the utmost respect for anybody – man or woman, boy or girl – who is brave enough to come through the doors at GA. For a woman to come in thinking it will be an environment full of men, it really does take something, although when they do come through the door I think they get a pleasant surprise, because there are so many people who are in exactly the same boat.

There is the obvious addiction to gambling. People continue to bet for different reasons. Some think if they keep punting then their luck will eventually change. There are others who get the occasional win who also think that big win is not too far away, or because they think gambling is the only thing that makes them happy. Personal circumstances also play a part in over-coming gambling problems, some individuals keep betting because they are too embarrassed to own up to their problems and too scared to tell their family or loved ones, while there are others who don't have anybody to talk to or support them through the recovery process.

Gambling is mental as well as physical. When you go into GA, you will be asked if you think gambling is an illness. It is a hot topic in GA. Personally, I think there are different forms of illness. I have learned through my time at GA that when I started gambling I had opportunities and I made a lot of wrong choices, although by the end of my time I didn't have a choice because addiction had taken over my life. I have only learned now from spending so much time in GA that addiction leaves you with no choice. At least with gambling you can do some-thing about it, with other illnesses, your life more often than not is not in your hands. When you gamble, you have choices. The deeper you get in and the more the bet, the fewer options you have or can actually see.

I know betting certainly affected me. It made me completely paranoid, especially during the day. I was a wreck who struggled to sleep. The only time I ever felt safe from everything that was going on in my life was between one and seven in the morning. That was the only time I felt at peace with myself. The rest of the time I spent most of my life looking over my shoulder, worried about people coming after me to get their money back, or getting arrested by the police. I knew they would never come round to my mum and dad's house at that time of night, though, so I could relax a bit. That was how bad my life was. I was completely disillusioned and in a total meltdown.

I also struggled at times with anxiety and depression. The depression and the general feelings of unhappiness were what pushed me towards suicide, while the anxiety of making sure I could continually gamble was an almighty burden on my shoulders. When you are constantly gambling, it does cause stress – although many people will think that is self-inflicted. It can definitely cause a lack of sleep. It is also not uncommon for gamblers to complain of headaches, bowel problems, ulcers and even muscle problems.

There is no doubt that anxiety and depression are the main two side effects that can come from compulsive gambling. I have no doubt about that, I see these types of illnesses all the time at GA. But I have also witnessed first-hand what they can do to people who are not gambling. My mum has battled with depression. I have watched her suffer and deteriorate with it. It is such a hidden illness, and when you do see it at close quarters, it really can open your eyes to how mental illnesses can affect people.

When you are gambling, you are completely blinkered to these other concerns, and you don't see or realise the damage you are doing to yourself or the troubles of other people. However, when you do wake up to their concerns, these realisations are what replace the buzz of gambling, the thrill of a horse coming in at 20–1 or that fifth team scoring to get a football coupon up. They are what matter, and what bring you back to earth, but under the spell of gambling they all become secondary.

23

A LIFE-CHANGING EXPERIENCE

You don't need have to have any set characteristics (other than a betting addiction) to come to Gamblers Anonymous. There are doctors, brain surgeons, footballers, sportsmen, right down to people who are unemployed and signing on the dole. GA is there to help everyone with a betting addiction, people from all sectors of life.

When you enter GA, the first thing you realise is that you need to totally change your life. I certainly had to change as a person. I quickly realised I could no longer be the main man and the centre of attention. As a footballer, you are often put up on a pedestal because so many people look up to you. You are a role model and icon, and it does boost your ego. I probably let things go to my head. It wasn't until I stripped everything down that I got to see the real me again. It took GA to help me find myself again. GA isn't just about your betting. It encourages you to look at every facet of your life.

Every time you go through the door at GA it is an acknowledgement that you haven't gambled since your last meeting. At the start of every get-together, the chairperson goes round the room and asks everybody if they have had a bet. If you say yes, you are asked what made you gamble and how you are feeling. There is a lot of emotion at these times. People don't want to go back to gambling, but it is an insidious disease. Everybody can go back and have a fall. I have been lucky. I haven't put one bet on, but I know that is down to my experience and time in GA. I also know that I have to take it one day at a time, and I can't take anything for granted.

GA is very much a long-term commitment. There is no magic wand. You don't just walk through the door and everything in your life is perfect. You have to take a good look at yourself, your life and your gambling addiction. GA can give you the help and support you need to stop gambling, and it can also give your life a structure, but the rest is up to you. It is a case of taking one step at a time and then building from there. After I had gone a week without gambling then I targeted a second week and after I was able to combat my urges then I could look at changing my life around, to make sure I didn't fall in to my bad old ways. The good thing is I had people beside me who had experienced similar situations and knew what I was going through. There were ups and downs along the way, but there were always people to support me and give me a wee lift when I needed it. I know, from that first meeting, GA has been a big part of my life. I owe everything to GA, and it has become my world. My life revolves round GA and my meetings. For me, it is the most special place on earth, and unless you go there and experience for yourself then you would probably struggle to understand why. I have so many friends at GA and they are all really important people to me. They are all so different but in so ways we are all so alike – in the fact that at one stage gambling has taken over our lives.

Everything I have got is down to GA, from my business to my family life. I now have an amazing relationship with every single one of my family and Jac's. I certainly can't say I always had a great relationship with my family when I was gambling. Also, when I was a footballer, a lot of the numbers in my phone were from more like acquaintances, although I do have a lot of good and loyal friends from my time in the game. But since joining GA, I have met so many amazing people and now I have so many numbers in my phone of people who are genuine friends. Let me tell you about some of them.

Tony is my best friend in GA. His experiences and what he went through in his life have helped me and so many others. His therapy is the most powerful I have ever heard, it is just so touching. It starts with him walking away from his business and his family and leaving Britain and his old life behind just so he can attempt to stop gambling. He just disappeared and headed for Bangkok. He never even told his wife or family where he was going. He wanted to go there because it was one of the few places where he knew he wouldn't be able to bet or drink. It was the only place where he felt he could go and not succumb to the temptation of his addictions. But he struggled to settle in Bangkok, and from there he headed to Thailand, but he didn't really like it there either. In the end, he decided to travel to Cambodia, where he stayed with monks. He travelled round the country with them, feeding and helping the poor. Some of the areas they travelled to weren't even safe, and they had to be followed about by the army for their own safety. Some of the tales Tony tells from his time there are absolutely horrific, from people fighting for food to the heartbreak of a child dying in his arms. It must have been a real eye-opener; it certainly is to me every time I hear his story.

Travelling and living with the monks made him realise how lucky he had been and led him to the point where he knew he needed to change his life. He eventually returned to Scotland and left £20,000 of his own money to try and help the monks. He went back home and stayed with his mum for three months. He opened up to his mum and told her about his gambling and everything he had done in his life. He had hit rock bottom and from there he was ready to turn his life around. He hasn't gambled since. He is now a successful businessman, back happily married and a real family man. He is somebody I look up to and has so many amazing characteristics as a person. He is one of the most patient people I have met, while I am one of the most impatient people around. I want everything done yesterday. It is one of the faults I need to work on every day.

Tony is the exact opposite. He is so patient and helpful. He would do absolutely anything for me, or anybody else for that matter. He has so many qualities in life. He has also helped me so much in my business and especially in GA, even though I have been there two years longer than him. He is a close family friend. He also gets on well with Jac, and both our families now spend a bit of time together, which is good, since friendship away from GA is also so important. I try to tell people about that in our meetings – you need contact and guidance from outside, because GA can only take you so far. It isn't there for you every second and minute of the day, and there are times when you need to stand on your own two feet.

Tony tells his story in our therapies, and no matter how many times I hear it, it's always a tear-jerker. It doesn't matter if I have heard it ten times or more. I only have to look at the faces of the people who hear it for the first time to realise how powerful a tale it is. I can see people just sitting there in disbelief, open-mouthed and gobsmacked. I know what is coming, but I still shed a tear or two from time to time when I hear it. Tony himself still breaks down when he tells his story, and he has been at GA for more than four years. It shows the emotion will always be there, knowing where you were that first night you walked into GA. That is why I have my little bottle with that message in it, to remind me where I was, and that is why I carry it everywhere with me. I only have to take that bottle out to know I won't gamble again.

Tony and I joke about all the time. We are very close. I will speak to him at work and five minutes later it will have turned into our own personal GA meeting. It is these little things that allow you to strive to take your life forward every day.

There is another person who came into GA at the same time as me and who is another friend. He did really well but after three years he left and started gambling again. He had everything in his life. A wife, family and two kids who he absolutely adored. But he took a fall and ended up gambling with his business and life. He eventually came back to GA again and got his life back on track. I thought there was no way he would ever start gambling again after that, but he did and has had to come back to GA for a third time. That final time he plummeted to the depths. He had hit his rock bottom. There were other times when I thought he had been there, but he hadn't. This was a guy who had a really successful business but because of gambling he was sleeping in the spare room of his auntie's house. He told us how he would hold his kids and then he would burst into tears when they would ask, 'Why can't Daddy stay with us this weekend?' These sort of things pull emotional strings with me. He was lucky because he has managed to sort his life out and has his business partner to thank for keeping his company alive. My friend had taken so much money out of the business to gamble, and if it hadn't been for his fellow owner, then he would have been left with absolutely nothing, so on that front he has been quite fortunate.

There was another incident when one of my other friends at GA was on the verge of being sent to jail for fraud. He was up in court for embezzling £80,000 to £90,000 out of a company before he had even stepped foot inside GA. The way he has changed his life round since has been unbelievable. You would find it hard to believe this was still the same person. He had been in GA for more than two years and that was the only reason why he wasn't given a custodial sentence. GA gave two letters to the sheriff to let him know where he was in his life. The judge actually took the letters and said that he wanted to read them himself because it would give him an insight into gambling. The judge said he found them very interesting. When my friend went back up for sentencing it was the same judge and my friend was told that the only reason he wasn't going down was because of the GA letters, and he genuinely believed he had changed as a person. My friend had shown great remorse and if it hadn't been for that and the support of GA then he would have found himself behind bars. The judge also said that case made him want to find out more about gambling and the troubles it brings. It was a major let-off for my friend because if he had been sent to jail then it would have absolutely destroyed his family. He looks after his elderly parents, who have physical and mental problems, and if he had been sentenced then I don't know what would have happened to them. How would they have coped? That was the main reason why his case was such a big one for GA.

There have been some harrowing tales. Another of my friends, who is no longer in GA but who I still keep in touch with, tried to kill himself over his gambling addiction. He went into the woods and took an overdose, but he was lucky because a man had been out walking and found him. If it hadn't been for that man's intervention, then my friend wouldn't be here today. He ended up spending ten days in a coma, and his wife and his children didn't even know where he was. That is where gambling can take you: when life becomes that bad it can lead you to jail or death – the end of the road.

Another galling thing about gambling is that there are so many younger kids coming to GA. It is really, really sickening, and a lot of it is down to the crack-cocaine of playing these virtual roulette machines. It is not about horses and dogs. It is about these virtual betting machines. It is hard for me as I am always there to give people help and support, but I do find it difficult at times because I can still see they have so much further to fall before they hit their rock bottom. I wish there was something physical I could do to stop them or cushion their landing, but I am absolutely powerless, and when you see people fall it can be absolutely soul-destroying. It is very, very hard because you can't physically drag somebody through the doors and be there for them all the time away from GA.

On a Saturday there is also a beginners' meeting. It is for people who have been in GA for a year or under. I sometimes go down to them, and from time to time, I also chair these gatherings. I find it good therapy because it opens my eyes to where I have been. I see people who have had their lives wrecked by gambling, with these roulette machines and online gambling, things that are so rife in society today. When I listen to these people, it brings me right back to when I was in my big, black hole. It is gut-wrenching. I can take things back to where I was, when I broke my heart the first time I went into GA and told everybody where I had fallen in my life. When I told people some of the things I had done, like stealing money off my dying nana, some people found it so horrible, while others didn't even blink.

GA has helped me take control of my gambling and life. I believe I am a better person and now I want to help people avoid the pitfalls I have fallen down in life. I take a lot of time at GA to help others, whether it is by going to meetings or speaking to someone who phones for a chat. I am always there for people, and it is the same when somebody walks through the door. I want to grab everybody and speak to them right away, but I also know I need to give people time and space to find their feet. There are times when I get frustrated when somebody comes in for a wee while and I think they are on the right track, but then they disappear and end up back in their old ways.

It is hard because GA, like gambling, can also be an impulsive thing. For example, somebody might lose all their wages during the day and by the evening they think they need to go to GA. They will come in and will maybe pick up something, but the next week they will be back on the gambling wagon again. You are taught at GA not to be judgemental. You have to treat everybody the same and give them the help and support they need to try and tackle their issues. What I would say is that if someone wants to kick gambling, then the two attributes that person absolutely needs are passion and desire – and they need them in bucket-loads. I think desire is definitely the biggest thing. You need that to stop gambling, because if you don't have it and you just come in because you lost all your money, then chances are you won't be able to kick the habit.

For a couple of years, I initially went to GA meetings on Monday and Thursday nights. They helped me stop gambling. I never went back to betting, but I still had all the traits of a compulsive gambler. I still thought I was the big man who knew everything, and I never thought I was wrong. I had a short fuse and a real temper, and the way I spoke to people was also so poor. When I really stopped and examined my behaviour, that was when I knew I didn't want to just stop gambling, but I also wanted to build my life up again. It was about changing my life more than anything else.

One day one of my friends at GA said to me, 'Why don't you try a Saturday morning? You can see what it is like.'

Keeping in mind my desire to change myself, I decided to give it a go, and now those meetings are my preferred meeting days, mostly because of Neil. Neil runs the Saturday morning meetings. He has stood by me and been a big help to me throughout my journey. I am really close to him, and his meetings have become a ritual in my life. I love going to meet people, talking about what is going on in my life and being around those in a similar situation to myself. I am a lot more aware of things in life. My Saturday meetings have shown my deficiencies and highlighted what I still need to change about myself. I want to learn from life and discover how I can help others.

I also use my life meetings to try and iron out some of my faults, like my stubbornness or how I speak to people. I want to become a better person and I want to treat people and speak to them the way I would like to be treated and spoken to. There are loads of things in life that I have had to look at and change. That is why my painting business is probably doing so well, because it is all about making sure the customer gets the kind of attention and care in their work that I would give if I was doing it for my own family. Everything I do is to the best standard I can give.

People pour their lives out at GA. They are giving you a bit of where their lives have taken them. It can be very raw and emotional. I end up in tears most weekends listening to what some of my fellow gamblers have gone through. We talk a lot about emotions and feelings. Things like guilt and remorse are massive for me. I live with that every day and I do believe those are the things that will stop me from returning to my old ways. As I mentioned earlier, there's a saying among people in GA: You should look back but never stare. They say you will never move on in your recovery if you don't. I have to say I find that very hard. Guilt and remorse are the two main emotions that stop me from going back to gambling. That is what I base my recovery on.

No one will ever understand what goes on in a GA room. I can talk to anyone about gambling, but I don't think you would ever get a full handle on things until you have been in a GA meeting. I think a lot of the general public could benefit from coming to the meetings because they are not all about gambling, but also about sorting out your life. They are life meetings. I've told Jac that she would benefit from coming to a meeting. She is not a compulsive gambler, but she has traits, like everyone else, which can be improved on. I think most people in life could take something from our Saturday meetings.

I also take a lot of selfish pleasure from seeing friends regain control of their lives and beat their gambling habit. I know from experience, it's not easy to do. To see them succeed makes me happy, as it's a big accomplishment to get as far as they have and to thrive. Thinking they were in similar situations to me, watching their progress and being there for their many ups and downs, and seeing them come out on top as better people really makes me proud.

I also try to be a better person, to help others, and that is why I primarily go to GA. I just want to give something back. GA has given me so much, but seeing people turn their lives around is the biggest thing for me. I would say I take more joy and delight from that than I did scoring a winner against Celtic or Rangers. It certainly gives me a bigger buzz than any of my gambling wins ever did.

There is so much unity in a GA meeting. As a footballer, you get ridiculed by fans and the critics. They pay their money so they have the right to their opinions, but if only they knew what was going inside the heads of some footballers . . . When I played football, especially at Hearts, I lived such a false life. If people had known the trouble I was in and what was going on in my life, then I don't think anyone would have believed me. No one sees inside that facade. I might have looked happy-go-lucky, but I certainly didn't feel it. It was all show. I wasn't a genuine person. I can now see things from the other side, and now what you see is what you get. No matter what happens, that won't change. I will continue to be the person I am today.

A few years ago I went on holiday with Jac and I decided when I got back I wanted to get a tattoo, something that really meant a lot to me. I got the Serenity Prayer down my neck and arm. Anybody who has had an addiction and sees my neck, they always ask if I have had a problem with drink or drugs. The Serenity Prayer is a big thing for everybody trying to hit the road to recovery. It means a lot to so many people. It is strange because at times my tattoo has led to me having deep and meaningful conversations with complete strangers, talking about addiction or where it has taken my life. Other people also ask what it is and I tell them it is a prayer I try to adhere to every day.

GA has given me loads of positives: Time, a clear head to think and ideas on how I can spend and dedicate time to people without worrying when the next horse or dog race is going to start. I can try and help other people. I am just thankful I decided to give it a go. My therapy has helped to make me a better and more genuine person. I believe I will never gamble again. I am very confident and I would take the biggest slap in the face ever if I did go back gambling.

I have built my life back up again. I am in a good place financially and I am a much stronger person. There is nothing to stop me gambling, but I just have to think about my meetings and know what it would do to my family to keep me on the straight and narrow. It would kill them if I had to put them through that old nightmare again – especially my mum, though it definitely hit my dad hard as well.

If my dad hadn't intervened back in 2005 when I needed him the most, then the police would have been involved and I would have ended up inside, I am in no doubt about that, because that was where my gambling had taken me. I am and will be forever grateful to my dad and all my family for what they have done to help me get on top of my addiction. I have paid my mum and dad back the money I owed them over the last five years, but I know what they did for me was over and above the call of duty of any parents.

I was lucky that all my family stood by me because I have seen other cases in my time at GA where families have fallen apart when somebody has confessed to a gambling problem. For some people, it can come as a real shock and can even leave fellow family members scared or even, at the opposite end of the spectrum, angry and betrayed. I am just fortunate I have a family who wanted to help and support me.

In a strange sort of way, what has happened has actually brought me a lot closer to my dad. Our relationship has flourished so much since I stopped gambling and started going to GA. He has been like my best mate, as well as a father figure. He came on my stag weekend, and we have done things together that I would have never envisaged us doing in the dim and distant past. If somebody would have predicted six years ago that I would no longer be gambling and I would be this close to my dad, then I would have probably brought them a straitjacket and got them carted away.

My dad has been a big influence on me. He is always there to constantly give me encouragement and support in whatever I am doing in my life. He went to GAM-ANON, support meetings for friends and family of people who have a gambling addiction, to support me for the first couple of years and has been by my side for every single one of my pins ever since, which is something I really appreciate. You are handed a pin for every calendar year you haven't had a bet, and it is of massive significance within GA.

It must have been really hard when my dad first went to GAM-ANON because he went there and it was full of women, while their husbands and partners were opening their souls about gambling alongside me in the next room. He says it has been a big thing for him because he has learned a lot more about me, and himself, in the bargain. These get-togethers are to give people advice on how to help situations and what you can do to help people avoid the perils of gambling.

My dad also stopped betting for a couple of years, and that was down to wrongly feeling that his gambling had something to do with my issues. Nothing could have been further from the truth. He now knows I can stand on my own two feet when it comes to gambling, and he doesn't go to GAM-ANON every week now. He still does sporadically, but I tell him he still needs to keep going to give other people and their partners the support he was given when he first walked through the door.

He has also helped me set up my own painting and decorating business. He is somebody I look up to and I hope one day people might look up to me in that same way. I also look at my dad and the way he acts with my sister Nicola and my wee niece Kelsa, and the way he looks after my mum. Only since I have stopped gambling have I seen what a great man he is. I never saw any of his good points and strengths before because I wasn't really interested, I only wanted to gamble and blow my own life.

My mum has always been my rock through my ups and downs. In recent years she has had her own problems, but my dad has been beside her every step of the way to pick her up, especially in her darker days. My dad is the most important person my mum has, and it took me until after I had stopped gambling to realise that. My dad is central to the entire family and is there to keep us all together, regardless of whether things are good, bad or indifferent.

Overall, my parents have put a lot of trust and faith in me. I would never want to go back to gambling, but I also know I just couldn't do that to my mum and dad, two of the greatest people I know and who I am so lucky to have in my life.

24

FINDING MY REAL JAC OF HEARTS

I met Jac just over a year after I had been at Gamblers Anonymous. We were at Lulu, a nightclub in Edinburgh, and another girl whose partner was also going to GA introduced us. We got chatting and we just seemed to click. We spoke at great length about life, and within a couple of hours of meeting her, I had probably told her everything I had done in my life, good and bad. I am surprised she didn't run a mile. It was a really emotional chat, and it is funny I had never really opened up to a complete stranger like that in all my life. She is one of the lucky ones, as she has never known me as a gambler. I also got to find out what sort of person she was.

If I am being honest, before that I was pretty materialistic. I didn't really look too deeply at people beyond their looks. I know it sounds shallow, but that is the truth. I was so superficial because I was more interested in appearances than anything else, but that is how shallow a person I was.

I never ever thought I would get married. I could never have seen myself settling down, and I even told Jac that during that first night because my head was still all over the place. I hadn't really explored GA at that point. I had only been going there to stop gambling. When I was in the full throes of gambling, I was never interested in settling down. I was maybe a bit of a jack-the-lad. Some people used to laugh and joke that I was Frank

McAvennie's love child because of some of my antics. I used to have a bit of the gift of the gab while out gambling, drinking and carrying on. Going to GA and turning my life around has given me a completely new focus and has helped me grow up and become a more mature person. And, the more I got involved with GA, the more I saw of Jac.

The more time I spent with Jac, the more I realised that she was the one person I wanted to spend the rest of my life with. We have never really been apart since. It has been a great journey, and we have just grown and blossomed as a couple. Jac has also been a big influence on me. It is down to her that I am a more thoughtful person. I think deep down I have always been a kind and caring person, but Jac really brought all that out in me. We both learn things from each other, and she is also really interested in my GA progress. If I don't go to my meetings, she is there to quiz me and ask me why I haven't gone. I always told her from the start not to let me slack off and miss my meetings. I know it is for my benefit, nobody else's. Also when I come back from my meetings she is there for me, whether it has been a good or bad meeting. She can tell as soon as I walk in the door what kind of night I have had. It can be really emotional, and it is good to come home and to be able to share things with somebody close to you. It means so much to me and gives Jac and me a real bond. That is why I always end the meetings I chair with the simple message: Go home and give your loved ones a cuddle because they are the people who stick by you through thick and thin. They are always there for you. It is a lot easier to make changes when you have people around to help you and support you. You also have to want to change, but there is no doubt Jac has been a big influence on my life.

There have been times when I have been really hard on myself. I am my own worst critic. I know the life I lived before, and if

Jac hadn't been there offering me support, I would have relied a lot more on GA because of how much I needed my life to change. I had to stop gambling, but there was a lot more than just the betting, as I have said. The person also needs to change. If you don't want to change your traits and the person you are, then there is a fair chance you could fall back into gambling again. I had to find a focus.

That is one of the reasons why I chose to write this book and I do talks and go round schools and football clubs, so I can use my own experiences to help others. If I can help one person, then that is great. I know it is not a great way to live life – needing to help others to make you feel better – but that is the way I have to live my life.

If I had never met Jac, then for me it would be ten times harder because she has seen me in some really bad and dark places. There have been times when I have gone up to see my mum and I have come back to the flat and broken down in tears. Jac has asked me why, and it is just down to guilt. My mum doesn't keep amazingly well, and I know deep down it is not all my fault, but I know I certainly haven't helped her. I still blame myself because I could have given my parents a better life and I didn't. Every day is now about paying them back. My dad doesn't believe in that. He has told me that I don't need to pay anything back, all he and my mum want is to see me flourish in my life and to continue with GA.

I do try and make up for the things I have done, especially with my mum and dad, and when Jac tells me that I have to admit that, I find it hard to hear. At times I also give her a hard time and tell her she doesn't know the half of it or how I am feeling, but after ten or fifteen seconds, I quickly come to my senses and apologise. There is no doubt she knows more about me than anybody else.

Jac is great. She is a fantastic listener. I have qualities as a person, but one of the things I am trying to concentrate and develop at GA is listening. People say you learn to listen and you also listen to learn. I need to listen and learn a bit more because my opinions are not always right. Jac is always there with an open ear and that is a fantastic attribute to have.

Jac always says that in a lot of ways she was glad I was a gambler and I have come through what I have, because it has made me the person I am today. It is just a shame I had to go to the pits of the earth to do it. I know I would never have become the person I am today if I hadn't been to hell and back. At the end of every pin, it is devastating to look back on the carnage I have cost and that, for me, is addictive gambling down to a T.

Jac, to be fair, is a beautiful woman, but she also has a fantastic heart in the bargain. I haven't met many people who are more caring and more loving than her. She is kind and caring, and family means everything to her. She has amazing qualities and values which I cling to and learn from. She does everything for me and for her family as well. She goes out of her way to see that my business is doing well and I am okay. She has built her life round her family and that is the way it should be. My family is now my whole world and to have somebody like Jac beside me is just absolutely amazing.

She dotes on her mum and dad, Margaret and Neil Boyle. Her mum has had a really hard time with cancer, but thankfully she has battled through that and is now keeping well. Margaret, like Jac, is such a lovely person, as is Neil. I see a lot of my own dad in Neil because he is so placid and laid-back. They are a very kind, caring family and amazing people, especially when their grandchildren are around. I am so lucky to have met people like that outside of my own family. I have never really been involved or got to know people like that because of gambling and what it had turned me into.

Having Neil and Margaret behind us is like having a second mum and dad to me, and without both sets of parents, we would have struggled to do all the things we did on our wedding day. Their support during our time together has been overwhelming.

Jac and I went out together for a couple of years before deciding to tie the knot. I took her down to Blackpool because she loves it there. I decided that was the place where I would ask her to marry me. Before that, though, I went and asked her dad, and I have to say that was a daunting affair. That was nothing to do with Neil. It was more down to the fact I never thought I'd get married. I spoke to her dad, told him that Jac made me so happy and that I wanted to ask him if he would give me her hand in marriage. Thankfully, he agreed, because I hate to think what I would have done if he had refused.

I had everything planned for our big day in Blackpool. I went away to a restaurant in the afternoon and I told him I would be coming back that evening to propose. I even had Take That playing in the background. I had everything planned and my proposal all scripted, word for word. Then when I walked into the restaurant I turned into a jibbering wreck. I babbled on for about ten seconds before I started crying and I finally said to Jac, 'Do you want to get engaged?' I fell apart, I knew I would get emotional, but I didn't think I would be as bad as that. I am a pretty emotional guy, and I take a lot of things to heart as before I didn't care much about anything. Emotions were almost alien, because everything was about gambling. I have found a different side to myself now; I can now sit and start crying watching *X-Factor* so that shows how much I have changed.

Eventually, I was able to tell Jac what she meant to me and how she was so special and everything I ever wanted in a wife and soul mate. I went down on one knee and the whole restaurant got up and starting clapping, so that made me a hundred times more nervous. Thankfully, Jac said yes and made me the happiest man in the world. It was just as well she agreed, because the restaurant owner came and asked me what Jac had said, and I would have been absolutely mortified if she had said no. Jac was also very emotional, and it was a real touching night that will live with me forever.

Jac, in typical style, wanted to get married within a year, but I knew we had to save and get our finances in order so we could have the perfect wedding. It was a whirlwind, but it was great because we were able to save some money up and all our parents did a lot of work and helped back us financially to have the wedding that we both wanted. We eventually got married on 18 June 2010, down on the Quayside in Musselburgh. It was the perfect day, and since then both our families have come together as one.

Jac has also read my GA therapy notes, sometimes just called 'therapy'. I have seven pages of notes from before I went to GA that document where I was in life. I sometimes take my therapy and read it in my meetings, although not as much now because I have been in GA for so long now. I gave it to Jac to read about a year after we were together. I went back through to the bedroom ten minutes later and she was just sitting there in tears. She said, 'I don't really want to say this to you, but I felt really sorry for you. I never thought anybody could fall that far down in life, and I really felt for you. I just find it hard that you were that kind of person and you have now changed into the person you are today.' I had always been open and honest with her, but I know how difficult it must have been for her to read my therapy just to see where I had been in my life.

We also are really very close to Jac's sister Nicola and her husband Nick. They have three kids, Elliott, Nathan and Alex.

We spend a lot of time with the children and Jac and I absolutely adore them. Nicola and Nick have also been really supportive of us, and from the beginning they knew that I had been at GA and the sort of person I had been. They are two very kind people and, like everyone else on Jac's side, they are really family orientated. If somebody isn't family orientated then they would be lucky to get in either of our lives.

There is also Jac's brother Neil as well. He is married to Elaine, and they have twins, Anna and Chloe. We love to go and see them in Rosyth. It is nice to have that warmth round outwith my own family. My life now is all about family, whether that is going to see my own family or Jac's, that is now the main focus of our lives. I try to do as much as I can for my mum, dad, sister and Kelsa and her family, while living a good life with Jac. She also has a lot of nice friends and that is because she is such a genuine person.

The icing on the cake for Jac and me would be if we were able to have a child of our own. It would be great to have a child because it would make our marriage and relationship even stronger, if that is possible. I am sure that will happen, it's just a matter of time and patience.

25

LIFE NOW

As I mention earlier, I first started working with a local painter in Edinburgh when I was young, and years later – about a year after joining GA, actually – I once again took up a paintbrush and worked for another local painter, also in Edinburgh. It was soon after meeting Jac that I considered starting a painting and decorating business of my own. I discussed things with Jac and my dad, and told them my plan. They were both really supportive. I knew I would need help, especially financially, to get a van and all my equipment so I could get things up and running. I also knew I would need a few thousand pounds to get started, and yet again my mum and dad were there to help support and back me. Everybody around me did everything they could to help make my dream a reality, and after that I knew it was up to me to make a success of things.

Even now my friends and family have been there for me every step of the way. Jac is great because she does my invoices and a lot of secretarial and promotional work for me, which is over and above her own work. My mum and dad, as I have said before, have also helped me massively. Thankfully, I have made a success of things and over the last four or five years I have been able to pay them all the money they were owed back.

My friend, Stevie Curran, has also more than played his part in my success by setting up my company webpage for me. I have had so much work through my website and that has been a massive factor in helping to build up my business. It is good because it also shows first-hand the sort of work I can do. It has certainly got me more than my fair share of work.

In the beginning, I was determined I wasn't going to let anybody down and that I was going to work hard to make a success of things and to finally make people proud of me. I feel I have done that. I have been really fortunate to have built such a strong clientele base, and to be doing a lot of work for big companies like Ryden and Leslie Deans, as well as my small individual customers. The good thing is that a lot of my work comes from returning customers, so that shows I must be doing something right. Reputations count for everything, especially when you work in an industry like painting and decorating.

I have to say I love what I do now. It is hard to believe this is the same person who hated every minute of the job when I was starting out on my apprenticeship. But, as you know, a lot of things have changed since then – nobody more so than myself. Now I know that I have to do to be the best I can. It is also different because being my own boss, I know the buck stops with me. Working for myself also gives me a lot more freedom, and I would probably find it hard to go and work for somebody else again. I have worked hard to get to the position I am in today, but I have to say it has been a fantastic and worthwhile experience.

I had a young apprentice called Ross working with me for three and a half years before he left to join the prison service. He was a big loss but I can understand why he left, because at times in this business it can be quiet and there isn't the same money coming in. It can be difficult when you have bills to pay and a family to support. I find it easier to adapt because I now

know how to manage my money. I don't go spending everything I have because I know there will be times when I will be
quieter and I might need to keep some money aside. The good
thing is with my dad out of work he helps me during busier
times, although yet again he never takes a penny off me. I think
he just enjoys getting out of the house, keeping himself active
and helping his son.

I know I have done some horrendous things to my family,
especially my mum, dad and nana. But I have always loved
them, although at times they might have questioned that. At
times, even when I was gambling, I still loved them all dearly.
That was the main reason why I never went to Sheffield United
when I left Motherwell. I could have nearly doubled my wages
but I decided to go to Hearts, and the main reasons for that were
my nana was dying and my mum wasn't keeping great either.
That decision had nothing to do with gambling. I could have
gone down there and betted even more, but at the back of my
mind, despite my illness and all my problems, I wanted to be
there for my mum and nana. I couldn't walk away from them,
and I told Neil Warnock that as well. Even in my darkest days
I did care for my family, although at times I did have a funny
way of showing it. I still had the audacity to steal money from
them all, money they had worked so hard to save.

And they aren't the only ones I've let down and haven't treated
as they deserved. My neice Kelsa and daughter Emma, especially, mean so much to me, and I am so glad things are better
between us. Kelsa is an amazing girl. I now try and help her
and do the things I should have done with my own daughter
when she was younger. It is funny, Kelsa used to dote on me
because I would take her here, there and everywhere and also
buy her things, but I have now moved out of Danderhall and
my dad has knocked me off that perch. Nicola now jokes that

she worries about everyone else more than she does about me, as before I would have been at the top of her list.

And Emma, she should have got the same care and attention from me that Jack gets when she was growing up but, unfortunately, she never got that because my gambling took it away from her. That is not an excuse, though. You hear it all the time in GA how people have no relationships with their partners or kids because they are hooked on betting. As I know all too well, it is the people closest to you who you bring down with you. I did that all through my gambling days.

Back then I was young and stupid. Now it is all about what Jac and I can do for Emma and Jack, and what they mean to me. Emma has always meant everything to me, although I haven't shown it as best I could. I know both Emma and Jill see me as a different person from the one they used to live with. My life has turned full circle, and I have become a better person. Now I have a good and strong relationship with Emma. I know it was hard for Jac at first, but she and Emma get on really well now and that is something that is very important to me. It's also amazing now that I am a granddad and I get to spend so much time with baby Jack. We all love and adore him so much. Emma and Jack are a big part of my life and I love seeing the wee one, even though he is growing up so fast.

I have been going to GA for more than six years now, and I am in a better place in life than I ever could have imagined all those years ago. I am married, in a flat with my wife Jac, and I am so happy in life. I have so many people who I care about that are all still here and fit as well, which is also very important to me. I couldn't ask for anything more.

I try to base my life around honesty – that is the biggest thing to me. As long as I am doing good in others' lives and I have people who care around me, I can live life to the full. I now have an amazing relationship with my mum and dad. I have a wonderful wife, daughter and grandson. I also know they are all proud of the way I have turned things around. And now my life is no longer all about me. It is more about what I can do for other people and how I can bring happiness to other people's lives.

26

GAMBLING IN FOOTBALL

Gambling is absolutely rife in football. It is unbelievable. I have seen the number of top-level professionals who go to Gamblers Anonymous. Nobody sees it, but a lot of football people are aware that some of their players have problems and they are now trying to help them. I would go as far as saying that there is more than one major first-team player in every Scottish Premier League club who has a gambling problem. It is definitely more a trait amongst the British-based players than the foreign professionals because of the differing cultures. You would be absolutely stunned by the number of professional players who are in trouble because of betting and gambling. I know and I can see, as a former gambler, what things are like in football.

The players I feel most sorry for and worry about are the young kids coming into the game. I hear so many stories about their gambling at so many different clubs, and it actually scares me. It takes me back to the days when I was playing and gambling silly amounts of money that I didn't have. It doesn't matter if you earn £200 a week or £2 million a week. If you are a compulsive gambler then you will bet everything you have and more, money you know you shouldn't be doing. I have seen kids making £200 or £300 a week and then put it all on a Saturday football coupon, it is absolutely frightening. These guys are leaving themselves with no money, but they don't really think about the consequences because all they are thinking about is the buzz of gambling and the thrill of possibly winning money.

There are people in the game who, without question, seriously need help. Some of them have held their hands up and are receiving support, but there are others who are spinning further and further out of control with every passing hour. Gambling is the worst it has been in the game. In England, Gamblers Anonymous have the former Manchester City player Jeff Whitley, who does a lot of good work to promote and raise awareness. He takes the players at Wolverhampton Wanderers for an hour every week and holds a GA meeting. Gambling is so widespread in the game that you just wouldn't believe.

It is often said that as soon as you walk onto a football pitch and that first whistle goes then you are able to leave all your problems on the side of the pitch. Football can be an escape for a lot of people, but it certainly wasn't for me. I can remember playing at Ibrox. The game was still going on and I was too busy looking at the scoreboard at the half-time results because I had a coupon on. The game was passing me by, but I was more worried about my big-money bets than playing football in my chosen career for fans who had paid good, hard-earned money to watch me. Football was secondary.

I do believe that unless you understand the addiction and the problem, then you are powerless to control it. Also what it does to your drive, ambition and self-esteem, you would never believe. Anybody who has gone through it will understand where I am coming from. That is why I use my own experiences to help other people. I go round football clubs and do talks at schools and colleges. I want to give people the support and guidance I never had.

The Professional Football Association (PFA) Scotland and

Gamblers Anonymous are both big players in that. They are the organisations that first got me to go to clubs and bare my soul. I tell them what I have done, and it makes me feel so good. If somebody had told me when I was in the midst of the madness of gambling that I would be doing this now, I would never have believed them. I was such a lying, cheating, deceiving, negative and horrible person. It was all about me. I was the be-all and end-all in my life. Now I am trying to help others, even if it means bringing myself down in the process. If somebody can learn from my mistakes, then that is all I am bothered about. That is the goal.

The first club visit I did was organised through GA. I went to Hibs, and I couldn't speak more highly of Colin Calderwood, who was the Easter Road manager at that time. I knew the Hibs players all looked up to him, and to many of them he was like a father figure. I don't think I had somebody like that in my day. I don't think I could have walked into any of the offices of any of my managers and said I had a problem with gambling. I don't think that was open to players back when I was playing. Most of my managers would have laughed at me and given me a £10 to go and put another bet on. I think there has been a bit of a change because people within the game have become aware of how big an issue it is and how disruptive it can be to players and football clubs.

I have to admit it was difficult initially talking about my gambling in front of a room full of football players. I had done it in front of schools, colleges, doctors and nurses, but talking in front of a team of professional footballers was daunting and probably one of the hardest things I have ever done, especially with people knowing I was a former player myself. It was a nerve-racking experience and I really sweated over whether or not I could do it. It was a hard thing because, having played football, I know what it is like to have to sit there after training to listen to somebody talking about gambling for forty-five minutes. I know if I was a player now and still had the attitude I had during my playing days, my reaction would be that I couldn't be bothered with this, so maybe some of the players also have this perception. The good thing is that I have been in that situation and I can open people's eyes a wee bit with my stories and tales of woe.

After my talk at Hibs, the PFA Scotland approached me to do some talks round other clubs, and I thought, 'Why not?' I felt I could use my experiences to maybe help others and help players get the most out of their careers. I achieved a lot as a wee boy from Danderhall, but I know I also had the potential to do much more in football. I achieved what I did with little or no effort or dedication. Maybe if I had worked a wee bit harder and done a bit extra, then I could have achieved a lot more. I have done so many things in my life and especially in football that I have very little memory of because of my gambling. I threw my football career away because of betting, and I now don't want to see the youngsters or current players being idiotic and throwing away their careers the way I did.

I didn't even know until I started doing my talks and working with the PFA Scotland that footballers aren't even meant to bet on football. I thought it was okay to punt as long as you didn't gamble against your own team. But if you have signed a professional contract, you are not allowed to bet on any form of football, whether it be in this country or anywhere in the world. Basically the contracts are watertight, and if you are found to have gambled on a football match then clubs are perfectly within their rights to sack you and rip up your contract. So, basically, if Eric Black had known about my gambling at Motherwell then he could have got rid of me in a heartbeat. Clubs could fire a player for gambling, and they wouldn't have a leg to stand on. When the PFA Scotland tell the boys that, they look absolutely shocked. Most of them don't even know that is the case. Surely it is up to the clubs to make all their players aware that they aren't allowed to gamble?

I can't say one way or another whether it should be right or wrong for footballers to bet on matches. Players like to have a bet on football matches. I don't see anything wrong with that, especially if you are doing it within your means and you are not going to get yourself into bother. If people can keep it under control, then why not? I was different because I couldn't control my gambling, but who am I to deny other people some enjoyment from gambling on football? I would love to be able to be in control of my gambling, but I know it would be all or nothing. For me, there is no middle ground.

I have spoken to first-team players and youth teams, and I admit I was more sceptical about speaking to the kids because I just didn't think they would be interested. I remember what I was like as a young player, exactly the same. I have to laugh because some of the young kids are braver and more confident than some of the senior boys. I have had some of my toughest questions off the youngsters, like, 'When do you know you have hit rock bottom, and when do you know you have a problem?'

The talks at the different clubs are something I love doing, and it is amazing the feedback I get. When we visit clubs we normally do an anonymous questionnaire, which includes four main questions. The first question has multiple options for answers. It is: 'Do you . . . A) Gamble once a week? B) Gamble twice a week? C) Gamble more than twice a week? or D) Never gamble at all?' Other questions asked are 'If you bet, what do you bet on?' and 'How much do you normally bet?' I get to see all the feedback. There are no names on the questionnaire, but I can assure you that the feedback is absolutely staggering. The chilling thing is that it is kids who are answering the questionnaires. We only do talks with the senior players. The bulk of the kids filling in the questionnaires all admit gambling on football, and the majority of them bet more than twice a week.

I really enjoy doing these talks. It amazing how engrossing gambling can be. I know when I go into my talks that quite a lot of the players are sceptical. I can see that a lot of people don't want to be there and aren't really interested. When they first come in I see them fidgeting with their mobile phones or mucking about with their mates, but once I start talking to them and tell them what I have been through, it makes an instant connection. It gives me an enormous sense of self-fulfilment if I can see I'm only helping even just one person. I am baring my soul, but I could never have done that when I was gambling because I was such a lying, deceitful person.

When I played football, the boys were all away by two o'clock at the latest. Now I think it is a lot different and players are asked to come back and do extra sessions. The young players also have to do college work and that is another good thing because you are learning about things and it is not just about football. If you are nineteen and you are thrown on the scrapheap, what sort of mess are you going to be in, especially if you have been gambling? Your life could spiral into a real dark place, like stealing, drugs or doing dodgy things just trying to fund your gambling addiction. It is better to have qualifications to fall back on. I suppose I was relatively lucky because I was a painter by trade and I could fall back to that. I had something to do, but there are a lot of others who don't know what the future holds after football.

Looking back, I wish I had stayed back in the gym in the afternoons and done more work and got myself bigger and fitter. The only exercise I was interested in was running off to the bookies. People will now say and think, 'What a waster.' I was, and I can accept that, but one day there will be somebody sitting in the same position I was sitting in seven or eight years ago. I have been a professional footballer and I have experienced the problems of compulsive gambling first-hand. I know how rife it is, and if my story can help one single person then that is all I want to do. If I can make someone hold their hands up, admit they have got a problem and try to seek help, then that would mean the world to me. I just want to use my experiences to help each other.

I was so wrapped up in betting that I let it affect my football. Surely, if managers want the best from their players then they need to help and understand them more. When you have a betting addiction, believe me, football is not high on your list of priorities. Some players and kids might believe they are not that in that deep, but a lot of them are in denial, just like I was. You really are putting your job on the line.

I have to say I wish someone had challenged my gambling when I was a player, but nobody ever said anything to me. How nobody ever pulled me up, I just don't know. I am sure there were quite a lot of people in football who knew I had a problem. It was that bad at Motherwell that I couldn't go on team nights out because I had no money. I was on thousands a week, and I still couldn't afford to go out for a few beers because of my gambling addiction. I didn't have any money left.

When I was a football player, I never once wanted to move into coaching or management. Now I have so much drive and determination, and it is something I would love to do. It is something I want to do. I feel I have so much to give, and it is something I never gave when I played football. I firmly believe I could have gone and played at an even better level that I did. I believe that without a shadow of a doubt. I was linked with Everton and so many top clubs who wanted to take me places when I was at St Johnstone. I just wasn't interested in them. I was happy at McDiarmid Park. I was happy making a wee bit of money and then being able to gamble it away. Getting my wages and just blowing it. Some days I maybe won a wee bit, but more often than not the money quickly frittered through my fingers. The more I earned, the worse my problem snowballed.

I gambled on my own games, but I am just glad I never went any deeper than that. I sometimes wonder what I would have done if I had been offered money to help throw or fix a game. Would I have done it? I probably would have, especially when I was at my lowest ebb. I would have done just about anything for money. If it happened earlier in my career, then I still think I would have refused because I still had some decorum, but there have been a lot of stories of inside betting and match fixing. It is easy to see how it could happen because some of the players are in so deep and probably could be so easily tempted. What I would say is that in Scotland and the United Kingdom I don't think match fixing is an issue, although the same cannot be said about other leagues and players across the globe.

What I personally have an issue with is betting companies being the lead sponsors at sporting events, like William Hill with the Scottish Cup. They do a lot of promotional things before every round with players in their shops, wearing their t-shirts before most games. I don't think it is right having players, role models, in bookies glorifying betting. Footballers are role models, and kids especially look up to them. Youngsters might then think it is hip and cool to go and bet – and for me, that is wrong. It sends out completely the wrong signals. What happens if one of these young players was to end up going down the whole sorry path that I did? Football makes the gambling industry a lot of money, but how much good does it actually do for the sport?

I know that the majority of people who put on a bet can do it for a bit of fun or whatever, and that they won't go on to become heavy or compulsive gamblers like I did. But I also think we need to realise just how much the gambling industry has grown over the last decade, how much online gambling there is now and how much easier it has become to gamble in our society. And because of that, it's inevitable that the problems associated with gambling will also grow, so I think we need to act now to make sure this doesn't get out of control and also do whatever we can to keep young people as far away from the dangers of gambling as we can, at least until they get to an age where they're better equipped to handle it. Having been through what I have and knowing what gambling did to me, it's something I feel really passionate about.

27

FROM BEHIND THE BLACK BALL TO CAPTAINING SCOTLAND

I am the first to admit that I never fulfilled my potential when I played football. I know I could have achieved a lot more than I did. I had a half-decent football career, although with a lot more dedication and hard work, I am in no doubt I could have gone even further. If I had put as much into gambling as I did my football, then who knows what I could have achieved? I had a great opportunity and it was my own fault I didn't make the most of it. I certainly never got near the level where I could have played football for Scotland. Maybe if there had been a Scottish team for gambling then I very well could have been the captain or one of the first names on the team sheet.

It was a few years after I'd hung up my football boots that I actually achieved the honour of representing Scotland, although in a very different ball game – the sport of pool. That was another sport I was half-decent at as a youngster. They say if you are good at pool then it is a sign of a misspent youth. I can't really argue. I first started playing when I was fourteen or fifteen in Danderhall Community Centre. I used to play my friend Rab Banner. He used to open up the centre so we could play in marathon pool sessions. Rab always says I am some pool player, the best he had ever seen. It is funny because we still bowl together. When I tell him how my pool is going or what competition I am about to play in, he always jokes that people must pray they aren't drawn against me. I tell him that if he was to come and see me play, he would see how good the standard is and at times it is a step above me. The level at the very top is absolutely frightening. One of the boys I get on really well with is Scott Gillespie, who is the No. 1 pool player in Scotland. He is one of my best friends, and as a pool player he is awesome. He is the best player around and if you are an aspiring pool player then he is the man to look up to. I still learn so much from watching him play.

I used to be quite good at most sports when I was at school. I played football, bowling, badminton and table tennis. I also played a lot of table tennis with Rab at the community centre. I was a bit of a sports freak. I would try my hand at anything, but I played a lot of competitive pool. I represented Midlothian, and while playing for my district I lost out in the Scottish Under-18 and -21 finals when I was there. I continued to represent Midlothian when I was at St Johnstone. If I had stuck in, then there would have been every chance I would have got my Scotland pool cap a lot earlier because I was doing well and winning quite a few of tournaments. As with everything in my life during that period, my main focus was on my gambling and very little else. I wasn't counting my pool trophies. I was counting my winnings and then taking it all to the bookies to gamble. I would play tournaments at the weekend, around my football, and I was also in a Thursday night league. It was a good way for me to make money with a number of side games and wagers.

A good day for me would have seen me come away from training at St Johnstone, going to the bookies and winning £500 and then heading off to play pool to try and double my money. If that was the case then I would have cash in my hand the next day, but nine times out of ten I had nothing left by the time I walked out of the bookies most afternoons. I was just lucky I was good at pool and I was able to use my talents to try and win some additional income.

It is only now after I have been able to detach myself from all the nonsense of gambling that I can see what I can achieve in professional pool. There are hundreds of top, top players out there. A lot of them are better than me. I can play well in spells, but the top players play brilliantly all the time. Now, for me, it is all about the competition. If I win any money in competitions I put it all to charity. It doesn't make any difference to me. Money is now very immaterial. It is funny that I can say that now, because before when I was gambling it was the be-all and end-all.

I put my cue away when I was in my early twenties. The older I got, the more I pulled away from things. I used to play for fun, but I never took it too seriously. It was a laugh and a joke, something to do and a way to get my hands on some easy money. It wasn't until after I finished playing football that I got my cue out again. I got a bit of sponsorship from Willie McEwan and Tam Mann to back me on the pro tour, although I ended up blowing that money on gambling – though I was still somehow able to compete in pool events.

Bob Murray, one of my friends who I play a lot of pool with, likes to bet, but he will only really bet on football. He puts his weekly coupon on – nothing daft – but when the scores are coming in you would be as well talking to the wall. He goes into a different world because he is so engrossed in the results and his bets. I was exactly the same, if not worse, when I was gambling. Bob doesn't have a gambling problem because he is in control of what he is doing. He is also one of the most supportive friends I have, along with Craig Dargo and Elliott

Smith, but just seeing him in the zone when he is betting makes me laugh.

It actually reminds me of another story when I was playing in a pool competition at the Normandy Hotel in Glasgow. I had won a fair bit of money in the bookies earlier in the week. Bob, a few of my other mates and I decided to go to the bookies to put some coupons on. I remember I put two on. I waged £500 on three teams and £1,000 on another five teams to win in the others. My pals thought I was a Flash Harry because they were putting on £20 to £50 maximum. We sat there that night and I was waiting for both my coupons to come up. I pretty much went for odds-on favourites and Arsenal were the only team who were down. They were getting beat 3–2, but they equalised late on and I thought my coupon was up in smoke, but then it came through on the television that Arsenal had scored a late winner. I ended up picking up £7,000 from those two coupons. I have to say the thrill of hearing Arsenal had scored was the big thing, far bigger than the money I went to collect. I probably enjoyed it more because in a sort of sadistic way, I never really wanted to win a coupon easily. There was no excitement in that for me. I wanted to sweat and to do things the hard way. If my bets were all home and hosed at half time then that was no use to me because I would already have moved on to the next one.

Thankfully, when it comes to pool, now the only buzz I get is when I have my cue in my hand. It has only been since I have stopped gambling that I have really started to enjoy the sport. It has been a long time since I have been able to say that. I would say I am very average at pool, and I know I was very privileged to be asked to play for Scotland. There are so many players out there who are better than me who could have been picked. The year I was selected, my friend Bob never got picked, even though he was some player and had played for Scotland previously. It shows the standard that is out there.

Going away to play for Scotland in the European Championships in March 2012 in Bridlington, Yorkshire, was amazing. That was an unbelievable achievement for me, to be asked to represent my country for the first time. Scotland had three teams, the A team and a B1 and a B2 team. The A team included our top-ranked players like Pat Holtz, Pete Smith, Paul Harkness, Stuart Weeks, Gavin Phillips and John Brownlie.

The B teams included teams of eleven, who were picked from a fourteen-man squad. I was named in the Scotland B2 team, along with Lee Killen, Liam Dunster, David Rooney, Billy Stirling, Johnny Slavin, Stevie Walker, Graham Rae, Kenny Donald, Chris Payne, Paul Cruickshank, Hugh Thomson, Chick McCabe and John 'Tiger' Kerr. It was just a thrill to be selected and to be given the chance to go and show people what I could do. We had a big meeting and all the players were introduced to each other. I knew a few of the boys, but there were a lot of boys I had never met. It was a good meeting because the coaches, Kenny Donald, who is the Scotland manager, and Billy Stirling, spoke to us and asked us what we would like to achieve and do during the week, and what was expected from us as Scotland players. Then at the end of it the meeting, Billy and Kenny turned and said they would like me to captain the team. It was quite a surreal moment being told you were going to skipper Scotland. It was absolutely amazing and a real privilege. The selectors said they had gone for me because of my football background, and I had also had a spell as captain of Motherwell.

It was a great experience, and I really enjoyed it. It was a case of making sure none of the team let their heads go down after a bad result, and when I was playing I just tried to play well and to lead by example. It was my first time there and I was determined to be a good teammate. Also, on the table I didn't want to look out of place. It was a very emotional moment when we walked in, to 'Flower of Scotland'. The hairs on the back of my neck stood on end, and it was a moment I will never forget. It was a real honour just being there.

I played quite well throughout the course of the week and my playing statistics were good until finals day, which was pretty disappointing for me personally. We played Northern Ireland, Shetland, England and the Republic of Ireland, and we managed to qualify out of that group and into the semi-final. We drew Wales in the last four and they were the favourites to win the competition, but we played really well and thumped them seventeen frames to ten. I have to say after we won that match I got really emotional realising that we had made the final. It was such a big thing because there is such a high intensity to the games when you are playing for your country. I was just so proud of all the boys and the team. I wasn't at my best in the semi-final, but that was all outweighed by winning, and winning in so much style.

We ended up playing the Scotland B1 team, and I was really confident going into the final. The team and boys had played very well and had good stats, but in the final we just fell to pieces, and I include myself in that. We ended up losing seventeen frames to ten. Only a few of us played anywhere near the level we could. We all let ourselves down, and I firmly believe that if we had got the chance to play that match again then we would have won or certainly have got a lot closer. But I have to say the B1 team thoroughly deserved their win, and I don't want to take anything away from them. They played extremely well and had a lot of good, experienced players in their ranks, like the former top ranking snooker player Billy Snaddon and Gary Gracey. That team had also won the title in previous years and on the day they were by far the better team and deserved their win. What I would say is the final didn't have the same intensity as the other matches for us, and that was probably because we knew so many of the boys from the other team, and a lot of them I would class as friends; there wasn't the same edge. We found it difficult to distance ourselves from the B1 team. Beating Wales was the pinnacle for us, and it went to such a low losing the final the way we did. I know the team were disappointed and many of them will be back down there again in future years, and I am sure they will, like me, learn from that experience.

I look back and I am so proud of all the boys and what we did. The other good thing is that I also met some unbelievable people when I was down there. Freddy Williams was in the Scotland B1 team. I didn't know him before I went down to the Championships, but I got on really well with him and I now class him as a good friend.

Maybe I should have played at that level years before I did, but I was never too interested or dedicated. Thankfully, I can now say I have played for Scotland and it is a case of better late than never. Hopefully I might get the chance to play for Scotland again. I know it is all down to me and what I achieve through the year playing in my Individual Membership ranking tournaments. If you can do well and get a run in them and in the Scottish tournament, then it gives you the ranking points you need to get back into Scotland contention. I know I was lucky to have been selected for Scotland and I enjoyed it so much that even if I didn't qualify to play for Scotland in the European Championships again, then I would be more than willing to go back down as a non-playing captain.

I regularly play in competitions and now it is just a case of trying to do the best I can. I went away in 2011 to play in the Super Eleven's pool tournament. I helped Edinburgh lift the trophy, which is something I am very proud of because that is another tough competition to win and that was the first year a team from the capital had lifted it.

We were down and some of the boys were playing the card game Crash for money to pass the time during games. There was only a small amount being waged on the cards and I can assure everybody that I wasn't involved. I suggested the winner donate the winnings to Children In Need. Ricky Anderson ended up coming out on top and so he handed me another £5 on top and told me to put it to Children In Need. I was going to phone the donation in but then I thought I could try and collect a wee bit more.

I went to the venue where everybody else was due to play and started collecting even more money. I ended up collecting £280 from that initial winning, which was only meant to be £10. I found doing that quite humbling. It meant a lot to me. It might not sound much to some people reading this, but I was pleased because I probably hadn't done anything like that before in my life. Back in the days of gambling, it was all about me. Charity and helping other people were never really things that entered my head, unless the charities were Ladbrokes, William Hill or Coral. I felt pretty accomplished having handled myself as I did and being able to donate as much money as I managed to collect for a very noteworthy charity.

28

GIVING MYSELF
A SPORTING CHANCE

I am also back heavily involved in sport again away from my pool. I enjoy a bit of lawn bowling. I play for my local club, Danderhall Bowling Club, mainly on a Friday night. It is a big part of my life. People at Gamblers Anonymous tell you when you stop gambling you have to fill that void. Bowling was another sport I used to play when I was a bit younger and then stopped. I now compete regularly and I take a lot of pleasure from playing. I don't play for money, although it is still very competitive. I win a lot at bowling, not because I am good but because I am lucky enough to have some exceptionally good players in my team. I compete to test myself against the best and for love of the sport, nothing else. I don't play for prize money, I only play to do my best and to try and win trophies. I certainly wouldn't class a game of pool or bowling as gambling, especially as I would never put a single penny on any of my games.

I am very fortunate because a lot of my friends also bowl. I also play most weeks with the Scottish international, Davie Peacock. He is ranked amongst the top twenty players in the world. It is easy to see why because he is unbelievable. It is a real experience to play alongside him because he always tries to help me improve and become a better player. He has competed in the World Championships and has also been at the Commonwealth Games representing Scotland, so he isn't a bad mentor to have on the bowling green.

Playing alongside him has been a real eye-opener because the standard he plays at is absolutely phenomenal. It is good because it gives me something to aim at and to try and improve my own game and standards. I now want to be the best at whatever I do in sport or in life. I really enjoy playing bowls, but at the same time it can also leave me very frustrated because I am too inconsistent. I can be good, average or pretty bad. To be one of the top players, I have to be consistently good. Away from the bowling it is also good fun. There is a lot of banter, and joining up with the boys is something that I really enjoy.

I was also part of the Danderhall team Davie Peacock captained when we won the final of the Top Ten bowling competition in 2008. It is a tournament where teams of ten go up against each other in your local district, over a number of matches, in singles, pairs and triples. If you qualify for your district then you go and play against the best in Scotland. We did well and managed to qualify for the knockout stages. We beat the favourites, Denny, in a dramatic semi-final clash, which came down to the very last bowl from Henry Aitchinson and led to us all jumping about the green at the end like little kids. We then went on to beat West Barnes in the final to lift the trophy. Looking back, it was some achievement. There is no doubt it has been the biggest win that Danderhall Bowling Club has ever witnessed, and every single one of that team can look back on that triumph with great pride. There is still a picture of the winning team that hangs in the bowling club. Whenever I look at it, it always brings back good memories and gives me enormous pride.

I am also very much involved in football. I have started coaching, and that was something I could really have seen myself doing when I was playing. But times change, and now that I am no longer gambling, I have a completely different focus to my life. I used to play football for money to bet but now I have got involved in coaching because I want to give something back. I never hit the heights I should have when I played, but now I want to pass on my experiences to help others improve and become better footballers.

I had a short coaching spell at Berwick Rangers after Jimmy Crease stepped down as manager. I knew a few of the boys, including my best man Elliott Smith, and they asked me if I would come down and help Ian Little, who was given the manager's job, initially on a temporary basis. I really enjoyed it down at Shielfield Park. Ian gave me a bit of scope to help with the training and to assist him on match days. It was a good experience and a chance for me to get on the coaching ladder. Ian did well and got the job in his own right and quite rightly brought his own man, Robbie Horn, in as his No. 2. He said he was more than happy for me to remain and help with the coaching and the Berwick Rangers Under-19 team. I really appreciated the offer, but the team trained on a Thursday, and with a lot of the games on a Saturday, it meant that I missed quite a few of my Gamblers Anonymous meetings. I thought that was unfair because there had been so many people at GA who had helped me and I felt I was letting them and others who needed my help and support down. It was a hard decision because I wanted to stay in football, but I also know how important GA has been to my life and those of others who are still trying to find the road to recovery.

Things have worked out quite well I am now back in football management with the East of Scotland outfit Whitehill Welfare. My friend Grant Carnie is manager there, and he is somebody I have known since we were young kids at school. He asked me to help him when I was down at Berwick, but at that point I felt it was a step back because I was still in the senior game. I really enjoyed my coaching spell at Berwick and I missed it so when the opportunity came to coach with him again, I thought, 'Why not go and give Grant a wee hand?' I went down and did a couple of sessions with Grant and the team, and I have to say I really enjoyed it. I also get on well with Grant. He picks the team and selects the tactics, but I speak to the players just before kick-off and when they come back in as well. It is good that Grant and I are so close and have a great working relationship because we have similar philosophies on how the game should be played. It is a real team affair, we work well together and we are just hoping we can bring a bit of success to Whitehill. It would be great if we could guide them into the Scottish Cup against some of the country's senior teams.

The East of Scotland league is also pretty strong, although we are one of the top teams in the league, along with Spartans, who have a lot more financial backing than the rest of the teams – Gretna, Edinburgh City, Berwick Rangers reserves and Stirling University. The league is also good because they pay a wee bit of money and so you can attract a decent calibre of player. The game also gets a fair bit of coverage in the Edinburgh *Evening News* and it is funny because they even put the weekly odds in the newspaper for our matches. Some of the bookmakers also take bets and give odds on East of Scotland league matches, so it just shows the scale of things you can now bet on.

We went on a good run after I came in and 2011–12 turned out to be a good season. We finished well up the league and closed the gap on Spartans, and we also won the League Cup final, which was a big thing. We beat Edinburgh City 2–0 in the final, with Scott McCulloch and Scott Gormley both scoring sublime goals, and that just capped off an unbelievable team display. There are some decent teams and a lot of the boys at that level could certainly step up into the senior game. A couple of the team actually did at the end of our first season.

I am now in the process of sitting some more of my Scottish Football Association badges to build up my qualifications and to help boys to try and improve and play at a higher level. I know these steps are important if I want to progress in the game. I also know Grant has ambitions to one day manage in the senior ranks and it would be great if I could help him achieve that particular goal.

29

THERE IS ALWAYS HOPE

As you have read, my life has been something of a rollercoaster. I have pretty much lived my life on the line. There have been highs and extreme lows – caused by my gambling addiction. It is also fair to say the majority of highs in my life came after I was able to kick my betting habit.

It is just such a shame that compulsive gamblers have to go to the depths of despair and have to take so many people who they care about and love so much down with them just so they can climb back up and become a better person. I had to do all the things I did, from the desperation of stealing to the lying and the deceit and falling out with so many people, and the guilt and remorse from those things are something that will never leave me, when I was lying in the gutter with everybody looking down on me.

I know it was no way for me to live my life. That is why I have written this book. Maybe some people will see a bit of themselves in my story and that will be enough for you to go and seek help. You might think there is nothing that can stop you gambling, but it can be done. There wasn't a worse gambler than me, it took over my life twenty-four/seven. Yet, I have stopped gambling and I haven't had a bet for more than six years. If you have the commitment and passion to stop, then I know Gamblers Anonymous will never fail you. If GA can help me then it can help anybody, you have to believe me when I say that.

It has been amazing to have been given this opportunity to write this book, although at times it has been hard. It has opened up old wounds and will have brought so many unhappy memories back to others. I have done a lot of things which have been absolutely shameless. While I was writing my book I went and did a therapy at Gamblers Anonymous. A combination of my therapy and recalling my old life led to me breaking down in tears. It has brought back a lot of stuff that I would never want to forget because I can now think of where I am today and how things have changed. I also have to state again that everything I have is down to GA. Without it I wouldn't have the life I have today.

Gambling has thrown so many negative and horrible things into my life but the one positive I can take from it all that overcoming them all has helped me to become a far better human being. I know I wasn't the greatest sort of person before, so in a perverse sort of way I have managed to use my past experiences as a motivation to make myself a better person. Am I glad I went down the road I did? Definitely not, although at times I do realise it has been responsible for changing and shaping my life and giving me everything I have today. It is just such a pity I had to cause so much heartache and pain to other people before I was able to turn things around.

I am so humbled to have all the family and friends in my life that I have. They mean so much to me, especially my wife, Jac, and all my family. I know I could have easily lost them, but thankfully they stuck by me and are still there today. They are everything to me.

I know there might be some family and friends who are maybe reading this book and they are worried or thinking about somebody close to them who they think has a gambling problem. How do you approach it? I would say every case is different, but I think you should definitely confront the person. It might help the person realise they need help and could be the point where their lives change.

The good thing about Gamblers Anonymous is that there is also hope and support there for families and partners. They can come and learn more about compulsive gamblers and what makes them tick in their GAM-ANON meetings. It can be a real eye-opener because it shows at times you are actually helping to feed the habit of your loved ones. You might think you are doing your best for them, but you are actually giving their gambling the oxygen to breathe and grow.

I know how big a thing GA has been for me. If people hadn't been there for me, then I would still be gambling – if I was still alive – and that is a fact. Everyone at GA has been through similar experiences and knows what gamblers go through. There is so much warmth, support and love within GA, but as an individual you need to want it. As I've said, you have to have the passion and desire to kick gambling – that is the biggest thing for me. I went through life waiting for that massive win or change of fortune, but if you are a compulsive gambler it never happens, because no matter how much you win it is never going to be enough. Unless you are strong enough to take on your addiction then you might have to reach the end of the road before things change.

I see new people coming into GA all the time. They are all at varying points of their journeys. You can change your life about but you need to want to help yourself. Some people will maybe have read this book, and said they have also done this or that. I have lifted the lid on everything, right down to the suicidal thoughts. I think everybody who has ever thought about taking their life over gambling definitely needs help. The help and support is out there. You can get support through various avenues like your own doctor, therapists and, of course, GA. You just need to take that first step on a road to a new life.

I have come a long way since I first entered GA. I know that. I have managed to stop gambling and to turn my life around. I have also changed as a person. I am no doubt it has been for the better. Personally, if it wasn't for GA and the guidance and support that people there have given me then I wouldn't be where I am at this stage in my life. I wouldn't be happily married, in our own home and running my own business. GA has definitely changed my outlook and made me look at life in a completely different light. I now know what friendship means, and I think that is the main reason why I am so close to my family. I have put them through so much. I definitely didn't appreciate them the way I should have when I was gambling, and that is something I am determined will never happen again. I can't change the past but I know I can influence my future and I will be there whenever any of them need me. I know that is the least I can do.

As for my own future, I just want to keep doing my best and hopefully my friends and family will continue to be proud of Jac and me. I will continue to put my all into our relationship and my work. It will be the same for GA. I will continue to go to GA because I know I can still improve myself further as a person and, more importantly, I can be there to help others and show they can beat the never-ending cycle of gambling, no matter how low they have plunged.

I managed to turn my life around, quite literally, against all odds, and if I can do it then anybody can. And believe me, it is a gamble worth taking.